JUDGING STATUTES

JUDGING STATUTES

Robert A. Katzmann

OXFORD
UNIVERSITY PRESS

OXFORD
UNIVERSITY PRESS

Oxford University Press is a department of the
University of Oxford. It furthers the University's objective
of excellence in research, scholarship, and education
by publishing worldwide.

Oxford   New York
Auckland   Cape Town   Dar es Salaam   Hong Kong   Karachi
Kuala Lumpur   Madrid   Melbourne   Mexico City   Nairobi
New Delhi   Shanghai   Taipei   Toronto

With offices in
Argentina   Austria   Brazil   Chile   Czech Republic   France   Greece
Guatemala   Hungary   Italy   Japan   Poland   Portugal   Singapore
South Korea   Switzerland   Thailand   Turkey   Ukraine   Vietnam

Oxford is a registered trade mark of Oxford University Press
in the UK and certain other countries.

Published in the United States of America by
Oxford University Press
198 Madison Avenue, New York, NY 10016

Library of Congress Cataloging-in-Publication Data
Katzmann, Robert A., author.
Judging statutes / Robert A. Katzmann.
pages   cm
ISBN 978-0-19-936213-4 (hardback : alk. paper)
1. Law—United States—Interpretation and construction.
2. Legislative bodies—United States.
3. Judicial process—United States.
4. Statutes—United States.   I. Title.
KF425.K38   2014
349.73—dc23
2014003481

3 5 7 9 8 6 4 2

Printed in the United States of America
on acid-free paper

For Jennifer

CONTENTS

CONTENTS

PREFACE

My interest in the relationships between courts and Congress is longstanding. In my pre-bench days, much of my research and writing focused on the challenges of governance, on the ways that our institutions operate, and on the obstacles to and steps toward the more effective functioning of government. I concentrated on a range of subjects, including the determinants of agency discretion,[1] and how the institutions of national government—the legislative, executive, and judicial branches, and independent regulatory agencies—affect outcomes over time.[2] I viewed lawmaking as a continuum of institutional processes, interacting with one another in complex and subtle ways.

My involvement in interbranch inquiry was heightened when in 1984 Judge Frank M. Coffin of the United States Court of Appeals for the First Circuit became chair of the Committee on the Judicial Branch of the Judicial Conference of the United States (a statutory group of twenty-six federal judges, as well as the Chief Justice, that makes national administrative policy for the federal courts). Judge Coffin, who earlier in his career had represented Maine in the House of Representatives, called for a systematic examination of the full range of judicial-legislative relations—past, present, and future. He asked that I assist in devising and implementing the Committee's research agenda. In time, we and some colleagues created the Governance Institute as the vehicle for our activities.[3] The first product of that enterprise was *Judges and Legislators: Toward Institutional Comity,*[4] a symposium that brought together scholars, judges, legislators, and others to examine relations between the first and third branches. In the course of nearly two decades in Washington, D.C., I had occasion to participate in several efforts that sought to improve interbranch understanding. For example, I worked with Capitol Hill, most especially with Congressman Robert W. Kastenmeier, to develop a mechanism to improve communications about statutory opinions, a project aptly described as "statutory housekeeping" by Ruth Bader Ginsburg. Many years of close association with Senator Daniel Patrick Moynihan afforded me the privilege of becoming involved in matters dealing with Capitol Hill and the other branches. Two years before becoming a judge, I published *Courts and Congress,*[5] which represented my thinking to date on a subject that has since changed greatly.

Now, having been on the bench for fifteen years, I return to courts and Congress, with a focus on statutory interpretation by federal courts—more specifically, the work of construing laws enacted by Congress. For a judge charged with unlocking the meaning of an unclear statute, there is no magic formula, no satisfying mechanical application. The task is often much like trying to solve a puzzle. As a judge, there is no responsibility I find more challenging and stimulating than trying to construe the words of a statute, consistent with legislative meaning. In the following pages, I draw upon my years on the federal bench and my prior academic life of interdisciplinary engagement in law and political science. My recognition of

the important roles of both courts and Congress has only deep-
ened in my time as a judge. Having been a longtime member of the
U.S. Judicial Conference's Committee on the Judicial Branch and
having served as its chair, I appreciate all the more that judges and
legislators need to understand and respect one another's institutional processes.

I hope this book is of interest to my colleagues on the bench,
law clerks, legislators, legislative staffs, law students, students of
American government, law professors, political scientists, lawyers,
journalists, and interested citizens.

JUDGING STATUTES

Chapter 1

Introduction

Over the last twenty-five years, there has been a spirited debate in the courts, Congress, and the academy about how to interpret federal statutes, the laws of Congress. As a federal circuit judge, I spend a considerable amount of time trying to discern Congress's meaning in the statutes it enacts. Indeed, a substantial majority of the Supreme Court's caseload involves statutory construction (nearly two-thirds of its recent docket by one estimate).[1] The steady diet of statutory cases reflects the simple reality that just as Congress produces statutes, so too are courts called on to interpret them. This is especially true when laws are complex, ambiguous, or seemingly contradictory. When in 2012 the Supreme Court declared the Patient Protection and Affordable Care Act of 2010 to be constitutional,[2] the role of courts with respect to that legislation likely did not end, but in some sense had just begun. For in the years ahead, courts will inevitably be asked to construe the meaning of thousands of sections of the legislation.

How should I, as a judge, interpret such statutes? Should the judge confine herself to the text even when the language is ambiguous? Should the judge, in seeking to make sense of an ambiguity or vagueness, go behind the text of the statute to legislative materials, and if so, to which ones? Should the judge seek to ascertain Congress's purposes and intentions? Justice Antonin Scalia has fueled the debate, arguing that courts should look to the text, that is, the words of the statute, and to virtually nothing else. I respectfully disagree. Our constitutional system charges Congress, the people's branch of representatives, with enacting laws. So, how Congress makes its purposes known, through text and reliable accompanying materials constituting legislative history, should be respected, lest the integrity of legislation be undermined.

In the best of all possible worlds, the language of the statute is plain on its face, pristine, and brimming with clarity. Then, the job of the judge is generally straightforward. Consider this statute, which I had to interpret: "It shall be unlawful for any person to knowingly or intentionally purchase at retail during a 30 day period more than 9 grams of... pseudoephedrine base... in a scheduled listed chemical product."[3] The appellant in the case before me had been convicted of purchasing 24.48 grams in a thirty-day period. My task in reviewing his conviction was simple. Under the plain words of the statute, he violated the law.[4]

But when—as often happens—the statute is ambiguous, vague, or otherwise imprecise, the interpretive task is not obvious. Consider these statutes I had to construe. In one case,[5] the statute said that a court may award a prevailing party "reasonable attorneys' fees as *part of costs*."[6] The parents of a disabled child who won relief in administrative proceedings before school authorities sought compensation for the costs of expert fees. Are those expert fees compensable as "costs" under the statute? Or consider another case before me: The law bars suits against the government as to "any claim arising out of the loss, miscarriage, or *negligent transmission* of letters or postal matter."[7] A postal customer sought to recover for injuries suffered when she tripped over mail left on her porch by the mail carrier.[8] The question before the court was: What constitutes "negligent transmission" under the statute? Yet another case involved this issue: Under a statute, "[i]t shall be unlawful for any person[,]...who has been *convicted in any court* of[] a crime punishable by imprisonment for a term exceeding one year ... [,] to ... possess in or affecting commerce, any firearm or ammunition ... which has been shipped or transported in interstate or foreign commerce."[9] Does the language "convicted in any court" mean any prior conviction in any court anywhere in the world, or does it only apply to convictions in courts of the United States?[10] How a judge interprets statutes—sticking only to the text when the language is ambiguous, or going beyond the text to other aids to discerning meaning, such as legislative materials—is of fundamental importance. The methodology of interpretation can affect the outcome, and thus whether the law has been construed consistently with Congress's meaning, at least to the degree that it can be divined.

Not only have these questions sparked considerable discussion within the federal judiciary itself; congressional hearings have also been devoted to the subject.[11] At confirmation hearings, senators probe judicial nominees, asking for their views on how they would construe statutes.[12] Law journals are filled with learned articles on statutory construction.[13] When Congress reverses a statutory decision of the Supreme Court, it's news. That was what happened, for example, when Congress enacted the Lilly Ledbetter Fair Pay Act of 2009.[14] The Act states that the 180-day statute of limitations for filing an equal-pay lawsuit regarding pay discrimination resets with each new discriminatory paycheck.[15] There, Congress heeded both Justice Ruth Bader Ginsburg's dissent in *Ledbetter v. Goodyear Tire & Rubber Co.*[16] and objections from many civil rights groups to the Supreme Court's ruling that pay discrimination claims under Title VII of the Civil Rights Act of 1964[17] are time-barred if the pay-setting decision was made outside the 180-day statute of limitations period. In words directed to the legislative branch, Justice Ginsburg flagged her concerns with the majority decision, noting that "the ball is in Congress' court."[18]

When the Supreme Court hears oral argument on high-profile cases, the method a Justice uses to approach a statute can also be newsworthy.[19] For instance, when the media covered oral argument in a voting rights case, it reported that Justice Sonia Sotomayor opined: "Some of us have—do believe in legislative history. Some of my colleagues don't...But at least one of—..." Justice Scalia pointed to himself, bringing laughter to the audience at the oral argument.[20] "Did he point to himself?" Sotomayor asked.[21] A few moments later, Scalia retorted, "Gee, if I believed—If I believed in legislative history, I would find that very persuasive."[22] In another case, considering a federal statute, the Defense of Marriage Act, that defined marriage as the union between a man and a woman, the media covered Justice Elena Kagan's inquiry about whether Congress's judgment was "infected by dislike, by fear, by animus," quoting a House Judiciary Committee report: " 'Congress decided to reflect an[d] honor [a] collective moral judgment' and to express 'moral disapproval of homosexuality.' "[23] Justice Kagan was indeed looking at legislative history to understand the statute.

Judicial interpretation of statutes has been part of this nation's constitutional experience from early days. In *Marbury v. Madison*,[24] the seminal case in which the Supreme Court asserted its power to review acts of Congress and invalidate those that conflict with the Constitution, Chief Justice John Marshall interpreted a statute, Section 13 of the 1789 Judiciary Act. President John Adams, among his last acts before leaving office, had appointed William Marbury as justice of the peace in the District of Columbia, but when Thomas Jefferson succeeded Adams, Marbury's commission had not yet been delivered. Marbury petitioned the Supreme Court to compel the new Secretary of State, James Madison, to deliver the commission. The Court found that Madison's failure to deliver the commission was unlawful and remediable, but did not force Madison to deliver Marbury's commission. Instead, it held that the section of the Judiciary Act of 1789 enabling Marbury to bring his claim to the Supreme Court was itself unconstitutional, since it extended the Court's original jurisdiction beyond what Article III allowed. The Court thus denied the petition. Although most scholars think Marshall's interpretation was a stretch, he avoided the dilemma of ordering Madison to deliver Marbury's judicial commission, which Jefferson would have overridden, or refusing to issue the writ— either way exposing the Court's limited power.

Over the past two centuries, the centrality of statutes to our system of governance has, unsurprisingly, become ever apparent. Statutes affect all manner of life, including the most pressing public policy issues of the day. They are the basis of much governmental activity—"the beginnings," in political scientist Charles Jones's words, "of life through law."[25] The number and diversity of statutes are enormous. Some statutes mandate particular actions;[26] others prohibit particular behaviors;[27] still others give considerable discretion to agencies to implement the legislature's meaning.[28] Some statutes affect states directly by conditioning federal aid on a local government's acceptance of particular responsibilities or agreement to implement particular policies.[29] Some statutes specifically provide for judicial review as to whether the law is constitutional.[30] How statutes are drafted—tightly or loosely—can give executive branch agencies more or less discretion to make policy.[31]

Statutes can address everything from the seemingly trivial to matters of fundamental significance.[32] Legislation is the basis for the administrative state as we know it. For example, the Administrative Procedure Act[33] established the essential framework for the regulatory process of the past sixty-five years. The Americans with Disabilities Act of 1990[34] is a civil rights statute that was meant to afford broad protections to persons with disabilities. The Clean Air

Act[35] and the Clean Water Act[36] are cornerstones of national efforts to protect the environment. Title IX of the Education Amendments of 1972[37] led to major changes in education providing new opportunities for women and girls in the classroom and on the athletic field.[38]

William N. Eskridge Jr. and John Ferejohn observed in their monumental work, *A Republic of Statutes*,[39] that some statutes transform constitutional baselines. Thus, the principle of *Brown v. Board of Education*[40] that de jure racial segregation violated the Constitution has been realized through a panoply of statutes, such as the Civil Rights Act of 1964,[41] which entrenched the principle that discrimination on the basis of race was unacceptable. Given the vital issues that statutes address—civil rights,[42] national security,[43] the environment,[44] the economy,[45] voting rights,[46] and gender discrimination,[47] to name just a few—how courts construe legislation is a matter of great consequence and thus attention. The phenomenon of "statutorification" of the law, as my colleague Guido Calabresi put it, is common to both the federal and state levels.[48] While my subject is federal statutes and their interpretation by federal courts, I realize that state legislative and judicial activity[49] is extensive and profoundly important.

When a court interprets a statute, the court articulates the meaning of the words of the legislative branch. Although, over the years, considerable ink has been spilled about how courts should interpret statutes, there has been scant consideration given to what I think is critical for courts discharging their interpretive task—an appreciation of how Congress actually functions, how Congress signals its meaning, and what Congress expects of those interpreting its laws. Although in a formal sense the legislative process ends with the enactment of a law, for the judiciary, understanding that process is essential if it is to construe statutes in a manner faithful to legislative meaning. Hence, Chapter Two focuses on how Congress works and on the lawmaking process as it has evolved.

In examining that process, I look in Chapter Three to how the legislators of Congress signal their legislative meaning to agencies—the first interpreters of statutes—and, another subject deserving full empirical inquiry, how agencies regard Congress's work product in interpreting and executing the law. That context should be instructive to courts as they interpret statutes. By understanding statutory interpretation as an enterprise involving other institutions, I hope to better address the question of how courts ought to interpret statutes. Against that background, I examine in Chapter Four two approaches to the judicial interpretation of statutes—purposivism and textualism. Chapter Five offers a view of three cases for which I was the writing judge and which the Supreme Court reviewed, agreeing in two, reversing the other. You, the reader, will thus have a sense of how judges interpret statutes, and how approaches differ. In Chapter Six, I discuss practical ways in which Congress may better signal its meaning, and how courts may better inform Congress of problems they perceive in the statutes they review.

By way of preview, I contend that the Constitution largely vests Congress with authority to determine its own procedure for the introduction, consideration, and approval of bills; and that Congress intends that its work should be understood through its established institutional processes and practices. Further, I argue that an important component of those institutional processes and practices, one which is essential to understanding statutes enacted by Congress, is legislative history, for example, committee and conference committee reports that accompany legislative text. Agencies well appreciate and are responsive to Congress's perspective that such materials are essential to construing statutes. What follows, then, reinforces my view that a purely textualist approach, which maintains that judges should essentially restrict themselves to the words of the statute, is inadequate when interpreting ambiguous laws. Respecting Congress's work product not only makes it more likely that courts will interpret the law in a manner consistent with legislative purposes, but also, as Justice Stephen Breyer has written, that Congress will perceive the courts as productive partners rather than as meddlers substituting their own preferences for that of the legislative branch.[50] Indeed, as I will show, it is a bipartisan institutional perspective within Congress that courts should be attentive to the legislature's work product.

Chapter 2

Congress and the Lawmaking Process

In providing a basic framework about the structure of government, the founders of our Constitution prescribed little about the internal workings of institutions themselves. They did, however, conceive of governance as a process of interaction among institutions at the federal level—legislative, executive, and judicial branches—and between the federal and state levels. James Madison and the other founders envisioned that each institution would have its own structure, purposes, and interests. The members of each branch would have the self-interest to resist the other branches' encroachments upon their prerogatives; yet, these institutions would in practice operate interdependently. And that system—characterized by the constructive tension arising both from the separation of powers as well as from institutional interdependence—would produce informed and deliberative outcomes. Although each institutional element would have its own structures, workways, interests, and purposes, together those parts would yield a balanced system. Senator Daniel Patrick Moynihan, a great mentor of mine, remarked on "the degree to which the founders of this nation thought about *government*."[1] It was to the institutions of government, he observed, that they "looked to confine and to moderate" the political struggle that the founders feared.[2]

That the Constitution's first article, Article I, begins with a description of legislative power speaks to the importance that the framers attached to Congress in the constitutional scheme. Congress is the engine of statutes. The Constitution defines the powers of the legislative branch, the qualifications and terms of members, the circumstances in which legislators may be held to account for their speech and actions, the presentment of enacted bills to the President, and the requirements for overturning presidential vetoes. Madison asserted that the legislative institution should be designed so that legislators would "study...the comprehensive interests of their country,"[3] as well as more immediate needs. *The Federalist* argued that the legislative branch needed to develop procedures so that its members would develop specialized competence and experience devising "a succession of well-chosen and well-connected measures."[4] As envisioned, the legislative body should have a relatively stable composition, with its members acquiring thorough mastery of the public business over time.[5] Madison cautioned:

> It will be of little avail to the people that the laws are made by men of their own choice, if the laws be so voluminous that they cannot be read, or so incoherent that they cannot be understood; if they be repealed or revised before they are promulgated, or undergo such incessant changes that no man who knows what the law is to-day can guess what it will be to-morrow.[6]

But the Constitution hardly delineated how the lawmaking process was to be organized within each chamber. It limited instruction to a few clauses, such as: "The House of Representatives shall chuse their Speaker and other Officers";[7] "The Vice President of the United States shall be President of the Senate, but shall have no Vote, unless they be equally divided";[8] "Each house may determine the Rules of its Proceedings, punish its Members for disorderly Behaviour, and, with the Concurrence of two-thirds, expel a Member";[9] "Each house shall keep a Journal of its Proceedings";[10] "Neither house, during the Session of Congress, shall without the Consent of the other, adjourn for more than three days, nor to any other Place than that in which the two Houses shall be sitting";[11] "All Bills for raising Revenue shall originate in the House of Representatives;[12] "They [Senators and Representatives] shall in all Cases, except Treason, Felony and Breach of the Peace, be privileged from Arrest during their Attendance at the Session of the respective Houses, and in going to and returning from the same; and for any Speech or Debate in either House, they shall be questioned in any other Place."[13]

Beyond these words, it was up to succeeding Congresses to determine their lawmaking processes. The framers who lived through the frailties of the Articles of Confederation thought that through the institutional learning that would come with time, the branches could best craft the procedures which would enable effective governance. As Gouverneur Morris of New York wrote about the Constitution: "Nothing human can be perfect.... Surrounded by difficulties, we did the best we could; leaving it with those who should come after us to take counsel from experience...."[14] And, in thinking about the first Congresses, which would create those initial processes, the framers might very well have felt that the task was manageable because the legislature's universe was small and thus more conducive to deliberation—a mere sixty-five members in the House and twenty-six in the Senate in the first Congress.[15]

Since the early nineteenth century, congressional committees have been central to lawmaking. Without committees, Congress could not function. By the mid-1820s, each legislative chamber had established standing committees that could expect that bills within their substantive jurisdiction would be referred to them.[16] In 1885, a young scholar, Woodrow Wilson, wrote: "Congress in session is Congress on public exhibition, whilst Congress in its committee rooms is Congress at work."[17] Richard F. Fenno, Jr., a modern observer, commented that members seek committee assignments that fit with their policy interests and constituent concerns.[18] The committee system can channel the pursuit of the individual interest of legislators to the good of Congress itself. Political scientist and Congressman David Price observed: "The committee system ... accommodates the aspirations of disparate members but also represents a corrective of sorts to congressional individualism—a means of bringing expertise and attention to bear on the legislature's task in a more concerted fashion than the free enterprise of individual members could accomplish."[19]

Congressional staffs, on committees or in the personal offices of legislators, assist members in their legislative work in every facet of activity.[20] Today there are some 130 standing committees and subcommittees of various kinds in the House and 98 in the Senate.[21] Some committees are authorizing committees, charged with making substantive policy as well as recommending spending levels to fund programs in their jurisdiction. Appropriations committees, responsible for determining how much money will be allocated to those programs and providing directions and restrictions as to how it is spent, can very much affect policy through the power of the purse. As part of the lawmaking function, committees examine how laws are being implemented through their oversight of the executive branch (and, to a lesser degree, oversight of the administration of the judicial branch). Because so many issues encompass cross-cutting areas of concern, committee jurisdictional categories can make lawmaking difficult. Hence, with greater frequency, especially in the House of Representatives, alternative arrangements assist or even supplant existing committee processes—for example, multi-committee arrangements, task forces, leadership-organized panels, outside blue-ribbon commissions, and "high level 'summit' conferences between legislative leaders and the executive branch."[22] From time to time, in the effort to strengthen its institutional capacity to perform its role as a coequal branch of government,[23] Congress will examine and make changes in its operations; one such effort I recall firsthand, having testified before a joint committee on the organization of Congress.[24]

Congressional decisionmaking is the product of multiple decision points; it is the product of both centrifugal and centripetal forces. The latter is characterized by the decentralization of the committee system, and the former by efforts towards centralization, leadership at the top, and party discipline. Judge Coffin, a former legislator, once noted: "What complicates matters is that both movements coexist today, something like the various shiftings of the tectonic plates underlying the continents."[25] Many factors account for ambiguous or vague legislation: the difficulty of foreseeing all problems; the often inherent imprecisions of language itself; the legislature's decision to identify an issue generally and then to delegate the issue to the executive branch for resolution; and the nature of coalition politics which, in cobbling together the necessary majority, may yield legislation that is deliberately vague and ambiguous. Congressional organization—with its many decision points—can frustrate coherent decisionmaking, producing muddy statutory language. And political polarization, partisanship, and gridlock further complicate deliberation and the task of passing laws that are plainly understood.[26]

Each chamber has its own rules of procedure for referring legislation to committees and calling up measures for floor consideration. The House's rules and procedures are far more extensive than the Senate's. The Senate, owing to its smaller membership, is generally more flexible than the House in relaxing standing rules in order to accommodate the interests of individual Senators.[27] Drawing upon the invaluable compilation of vital congressional statistics produced by political scientists Norman J. Ornstein, Thomas E. Mann, Michael J. Malbin, and Andrew Rugg,[28] I offer this snapshot of the 111th Congress (2009–2010) and 112th Congress (2011–2012) to give a sense of the congressional institution. In the 111th Congress, 383 public bills were enacted, with a total of 7,617 pages, averaging 19.89 pages per statute.[29] In the House of Representatives, 6,677 bills were introduced (including joint resolutions), and 861 passed, with a .129 ratio of bills passed to bills introduced.[30] In the Senate, 4,101 bills were introduced and 176 bills passed, with a ratio of .043 bills passed to bills introduced.[31] Additionally, the Senate held 2,374 committee and subcommittee hearings.[32] In the 112th Congress, with 2012 being an election year and members spending less time in Washington, D.C., and more on the campaign trail, 283 public bills were enacted, with a total of 4,415 pages, averaging 15.60 pages per statute.[33] In the House of Representatives, 6,845 bills were introduced (including joint resolutions), and 561 passed, with a .082 ratio of bills passed to bills introduced.[34] In the Senate, 3,767 bills were introduced and 364 bills passed, with a ratio of .097 bills passed to bills introduced.[35] In recent decades, Congress has more frequently enacted legislation through large omnibus bills or resolutions, packing together a wide range of disparate issues.[36] The omnibus mechanism is a departure from the traditional approach of handling individual pieces of legislation.[37] In part, Congress uses omnibus bills to facilitate passage of overdue measures.[38] For example, in 2009, 2010, 2011, and 2014, Congress packaged appropriations bills into a single omnibus bill, reducing opportunities for further delay as opposed to considering each bill individually. Because it is generally subject to an up-and-down vote, the massive omnibus bill masks differences over contentious measures included in the legislation that might not have passed if considered individually as stand-alone bills.[39]

Congressional life is marked by incredible pressure—such as the pressures of the permanent campaign for reelection,[40] raising funds, balancing work in Washington and time in the district, balancing committee and floor work in an environment of increasing polarization, and balancing work and family responsibilities. It is also now more intense than in the past. Consider these statistics: In 1955, the number of recorded votes in the House was 147;[41] in the 111th Congress (2009–2010), it was 991 and 664 respectively;[42] and in the 112th Congress (2011–2012), it was 949 and 658 respectively.[43] In 1955, the number of recorded votes in the Senate was 88;[44] in the 111th Congress (2009–2010), it was 400 and 307, respectively;[45] and in the 112th Congress (2011–2012), it was 235 and 251, respectively.[46] At times, these votes take place in the dead of night, especially as the legislative session moves at a frenetic pace to recess or end of the session. In 1955–1956, Congress was in session 227 days; from 2007 to 2012, the average was 323 days.[47] In the House, the session day consisted of an average of 7.4 and 5.3 hours per day in the 111th and 112th Congress, respectively,[48] as compared to 4.1 hours per day in 1955–1956.[49] In the Senate, the session day consisted of 7.1 and 6.3 hours per day in the 111th and 112th Congress, respectively,[50] as compared to 6.1 hours per day in 1955–1956.[51] In 1955–1956, the average total of committee assignments for members of the House was 3.0;[52] in 2011–2012, it was 5.3 (1.7 standing committee assignments, 3.4 subcommittee assignments, and .20 other committee assignments).[53] Similarly, in the Senate, the average number of committee assignments was 7.9 in 1955–1956;[54] in 2011–2012, it was 12.9 (3.4 standing committee assignments, 8.6 subcommittee assignments, and .9 other committee assignments).[55]

The key point is that the expanding, competing demands on legislators' time reduce opportunities for reflection and deliberation.[56] In that circumstance, beyond the work of their own committees of which legislators have direct knowledge, members operate in a system in which they rely on the work of colleagues on other committees.[57] Members of Congress accept the trustworthiness of statements made by their colleagues on other committees, especially those charged with managing the bill, about what the proposed legislation means. They cannot read every word of the bills they vote upon, and, indeed, reading every word is often not particularly instructive, to the degree bills contain language amending the United States Code or enacted statutes. For example, a legislator unfamiliar with the Hobby Protection Act in its codified or statutory version might have a hard time understanding this provision in a bill that the House adopted in July 2013:

> The Hobby Protection Act (15 U.S.C. § 2101 *et seq.*) is amended—
> (1) in section 2—
>> (A) in subsection (b), by inserting ", or the sale in commerce" after "distribution in commerce";
>> (B) by redesignating subsection (d) as subsection (e) and inserting after subsection (c) the following:
>> "(d) Provision of Assistance or Support—It shall be a violation of subsection (a) or (b) for a person to provide substantial assistance or support to any manufacturer, importer, or seller if that person knows or should have known that the manufacturer, importer, or seller is engaged in any act or practice that violates subsection (a) or (b)."; and
>> (C) in subsection (e) (as so redesignated), by striking "and (b)" and inserting "(b), and (d)";

(2) in section 3—

    (A) by striking "If any person" and inserting "(a) In General—If any person";

    (B) by striking "or has an agent" and inserting ", has an agent, transacts business, or wherever venue is proper under section 1391 of title 28, United States Code"; and

    (C) by adding at the end the following:

        "(b) Trademark Violations—If the violation of section 2 (a) or (b) or a rule under section 2(c) also involves unauthorized use of registered trademarks belonging to a collectibles certification service, the owner of such trademarks shall have, in addition to the remedies provided in subsection (a), all rights provided under sections 34, 35, and 36 of the Trademark Act of 1946 (15 U.S.C. 1116, 1117, and 1118) for violations of such Act.";....[58]

Legislators and their staffs become educated about the bill by reading the materials produced by the committees and conference committees from which the proposed legislation emanates. These materials include, for example, committee reports, conference committee reports, and the joint statements of conferees who drafted the final bill.

Committee reports accompanying bills have long been important means of informing the whole chamber about proposed legislation; they are often the primary means by which staffs brief their principals before voting on a bill.[59] To facilitate deliberation, Congress was concerned from its earliest days that its proceedings be published, consistent with the constitutional requirement that a journal be kept.[60] With the advent of the committee system, reports of committee activity were delivered orally, but, in the House by the period 1830–1860, and in the Senate by 1900, it was also commonplace for committee reports accompanying proposed legislation to be disseminated to the full chamber so that members could have a fuller appreciation of the bills on which they were called on to vote.[61] Committee reports are generally circulated at least two calendar days before legislation is considered on the floor.[62] Those reports provide members and their staffs with explanatory material about a bill's context, purposes, policy implications, and details, as well as information about who the committee supporters of a particular bill are and about possible minority views.[63] Conference committee reports represent the views of legislators from both chambers who are charged with reconciling bills that have passed both the House and the Senate and presenting them for final legislative consideration.[64] Members and their staffs will also hear from interest groups—including groups they find credible—and the executive branch about particular bills.[65] The system works because committee members and their staffs will lose influence with their colleagues as to future bills if they do not accurately represent the bills under consideration within their jurisdiction. Indeed, staffers would risk losing their jobs if they were to mislead legislators as to the details of legislation and accompanying reports.

Although any legislator can introduce a bill, it is the committee of jurisdiction that generally processes the proposed measure. In drafting bills, legislators look to multiple sources. In his memoir, the late Senator Edward M. Kennedy wrote that "[n]inety-five percent of the nitty-gritty work of drafting and even negotiating is now done by staff," marking "an enormous shift of responsibility over the past forty or fifty years."[66] Ninety-five percent, observed veteran journalist Robert Kaiser, the author of a rich saga of the passage of the Dodd-Frank Act,[67] "might underestimate staff members' share of the work."[68] Committees are aided by professional drafters in each chamber's office of legislative counsel; these drafters are trained in the nuances of statute writing.[69] Although legislators and their staffs are not required to consult with legislative counsel, doing so is prudent because a poorly drafted bill can lead to all manner of problems for agencies and courts charged with interpreting the statute. Typically, a committee staffer will contact the office for assistance in framing the bill so that it is technically correct. Those who work as legislative counsel think of the committees as clients.[70] Their role is not to offer views about the merits of a particular proposal; it is to determine how best to commit the bill's purposes to writing.[71]

Not all bills originate from the committees themselves. Some originate with the executive branch; others from interest groups, lobbyists, businesses, and state and local governments. These various interests may assist in drafting bills as well, but not necessarily with the care that each chamber's office of legislative counsel provides. Not all bills are drafted in the committee; bills can also be drafted, or at least substantially revised, on the floor and in conference committee.[72] In the Senate, flexible procedures allow senators to draft bills in the course of debate. When bills are drafted on the floor, for example, the pressures of time mean that legislators do not generally check with the legislative counsel, and thus there is more likely to be problematic drafting language.[73] In conference committee, the pressure to come to closure and pass a bill can compromise technical precision.

A case study by law professors Victoria Nourse and Jane Schacter, focusing on the Senate Judiciary Committee, reveals that committee staffers are well aware that how they construct statutes will affect how agencies and courts interpret them. The staffers view their task not primarily as creating technically correct statutes, but as addressing political and policy issues through legislation.[74] The statute-making process, as legislators and staffs understand it, involves not just the text of legislation, but also quite importantly legislative history—such as the reports and debates associated with the legislative text. As I described earlier, committee reports and conference committee reports accompanying bills can provide guidance to legislators in the enactment process.[75] Legislative history accompanying legislation can also be helpful by providing direction to agencies as to how to interpret and implement legislation. Scholars such as James Brudney,[76] Victoria Nourse,[77] Elizabeth Garrett,[78] Abbe R. Gluck, and Lisa Schultz Bressman[79] have more recently shown how Congress operates within a milieu of rules, norms, and practices—including importantly the applicability of legislative history. The degree to which these norms and practices shape both the drafting process and also legislative expectations about how laws should be understood is not commonly known within the judiciary—a matter to which I return later in this book when I discuss judicial interpretation of statutes.

*****

What relevance does this whirlwind survey of Congress and lawmaking have for the interpretation of statutes? The point is a simple one. The laws of Congress are the product of often complex institutional processes, which engage legislators, staff, and other interests with stakes in the outcome. Having a basic understanding of legislative lawmaking can only better prepare judges to undertake their interpretive responsibilities. Additionally instructive to judges charged with construing statutes is how agency officials—also important participants in the interpretive enterprise—view signals from the Hill, including legislative materials. On to the next chapter about that very subject: agencies and Congress, and what courts can learn from them about the statutory interpretation enterprise.

Chapter 3

Congress and Agencies: Interpreting and Implementing Statutes

The debate within the federal courts and the legal academy—as to whether federal judges should look only at the laws' text in construing statutes or go beyond the text to legislative materials that accompany the text—must seem otherworldly not just to those in Congress and their staffs, but also to agencies charged with implementing the law. Through laws and lawmaking, Congress communicates to those who have the responsibility of interpreting and administering its work. Congress's immediate objects in that exercise are usually not courts, which may someday be called on to interpret statutes, but agencies, which more immediately grapple with the details of implementing the law. Statutes may express the sense of Congress, but agencies must translate that sense into action. As Peter Strauss observed some years ago, agencies are generally the first—often the primary—interpreters of statutes.[1] And agencies are constantly looking for clues as to what particular statutes mean. In my pre-bench academic life, I would try to understand the agency I was studying by marinating myself in the agency, spending a lot of time onsite talking to agency officials at all levels; the importance of Congress to the agency decisionmakers became apparent to me. As

Herbert Kaufman wrote in his classic, *The Administrative Behavior of Federal Bureau Chiefs*:

> The [agency bureau] chiefs were consciously looking over their shoulders, as it were, at the elements of the legislative establishment…estimating reactions to contemplated decisions and actions, trying to prevent misunderstandings and avoidable conflicts, and planning responses when storm warnings appeared on the horizon. Not that cues and signals from Capitol Hill had to be ferreted out; the denizens of the Hill were not shy about issuing suggestions, requests, demands, directives, and pronouncements.[2]

Congress and agencies share an understanding as to how to discern legislative meaning that goes beyond statutory text. In communicating with agencies about legislation, Congress has a variety of tools at its disposal, such as confirmation hearings, appropriation hearings, authorization hearings, oversight hearings and investigations, committee reports, floor debates at the time of legislative consideration of a bill, and other non-statutory controls.[3]

The confirmation process provides senators with a venue to press nominees to commit to interpreting statutes in particular ways as a condition for affirmative votes. At confirmation hearings, senators may seek assurance that nominees will undertake or refrain from specific actions under the statutes they are charged with enforcing.[4] The nominee who does not keep her promise once confirmed may incur such costs as appropriations cuts or legislative changes. Legislators also advance their views about what is expected of agency officials in the course of funding hearings (appropriations) and hearings about substantive bills (authorizations). Committee reports and conference committee reports accompanying legislation will often require that the agency undertake or refrain from particular actions.

Statements of floor managers, charged with organizing consideration of bills by the full chamber, can also provide direction in floor debate as a measure nears passage. Oversight hearings, conducted by committees with jurisdiction over legislation, provide opportunities for legislators to monitor executive interpretation and implementation of statutes and to take corrective action if necessary.[5] Similarly, committee investigations offer another kind of congressional review, as Paul Light has recently shown.[6] In their aftermath, legislators may, among other things, press the executive to interpret the law in a different way; or legislators may move to change the law itself; or, Congress can mandate that agencies issue reports detailing compliance with the laws as a means of checking on executive performance.[7] Through the Government Accountability Office ("GAO"), an arm of Congress which undertakes audits and reports of governmental agencies, the legislative branch conveys its concerns about agency operations to the executive branch.[8]

Apart from these formal means, there are other informal methods for legislators to make their views known to agencies. These include telephone calls and notes to agency officials.[9] Although almost three decades ago the Supreme Court in *INS v. Chadha*[10] declared unconstitutional the legislative veto—a legislative device whereby Congress retained control over executive branch actions without passing a law—committee and subcommittee vetoes continue to exist. Louis Fisher reports that since *Chadha* there have been hundreds of such vetoes provided for in legislation or through informal and non-statutory means, whereby Congress grants agencies considerable discretion in exchange for a system of review and control by the committees of jurisdiction.[11]

Legislators quite clearly view these various techniques as legitimate components of the legislative process and expect that agencies will follow their directives, not just expressed in legislation, but also in legislative history and through the variety of statutory and nonstatutory devices noted above. And agencies recognize the importance of being sensitive to the signals and directives that members of Congress send beyond words in statutes. Agency administrators appreciate that they undertake activities pursuant to statutory authority and that having a full understanding of what Congress expects helps the agency discharge its functions consistent with statutory meaning. Agencies are charged with implementing legislation that is often unclear and the product of an often messy legislative process. Trying to make sense of the statute with the aid of reliable legislative history is rational and prudent.

For instance, if Congress passes energy legislation with an accompanying committee report providing detailed direction to the Department of Energy, it is unfathomable that the Secretary of Energy or any other responsible agency officials would ignore the report, let alone not read that report. An agency's sensitivity to Congress's workways reflects an often intimate involvement in the legislative process. Executive branch staffers often draft bills that committees consider, and even assist committee staffers in drafting committee report language. In the area of tax law, for example, such collaboration is routine and the legislative history produced in tax committee report commentaries is essential guidance to the agencies.[12]

Agency responsiveness to congressional signals other than statutory text makes sense from a policy and good-governance perspective of trying to interpret and implement the law consistent with legislative meaning. It also makes sense from the perspective of practical politics. Administrators recognize that Congress is key to the institutional health of their agencies. An agency that is mindful of preserving its autonomy, budget, and responsibilities will be sensitive to fulfilling legislative expectations lest Congress curb the agency's authority and funding, through the statutory and non-statutory devices described earlier. Hence, agency staffers commonly consult with committee staffers in the ordinary course of business as to what actions the agency is contemplating and how it is interpreting the law. Agency preparation for congressional hearings will typically involve close review of legislative directives in legislative history materials. Any administrator who ignores a directive in a committee report, or in a communication from the congressional committee, may suffer the consequences at the next congressional hearing, if not before.

Attention as to what legislators and agencies view as the authoritative work product of the legislative branch is instructive as we consider judicial interpretation of statutes. Supreme Court doctrine indicates that courts should generally defer to an agency's interpretation of an ambiguous statute that it administers, as long as that interpretation is reasonable or permissible.[13] That doctrine is premised in part on the Court's view of agency institutional competence, the sense that because an agency is deeply familiar with the legislation it is charged with implementing, deference to its interpretation is appropriate. It is noteworthy, I believe, that in the exercise of its institutional competence, an agency is sensitive to legislative history. Judges, I am suggesting here, would do well to understand the methodology of agency interpretation of statutes, to understand how agencies use pre-enactment legislative history accompanying proposed legislation. They should take stock of that learning when they construe legislation in the wide range of cases before them, not just those involving review of agency interpretation of statutes. In arguing that courts can learn from agencies, I emphasize that I focus on pre-enactment legislative history accompanying legislation. But while a court's inquiry into legislative history is essentially limited to pre-enactment materials concerning the bill voted on by legislators, agencies are also sensitive to post-enactment signals of legislators in the current and succeeding Congresses. I observe that although there has been thoughtful writing on agency construction of statutes,[14] there is a dearth of empirical knowledge about the methodology of agency interpretation. I urge a full empirical inquiry across agencies.

It is, as I said earlier, striking that agencies, to whom courts afford considerable deference as to interpretations of ambiguous statutes, view legislative history as essential reading, but within the judiciary there has been considerable debate as to whether legislative history should be used at all. This discussion has taken place in a vacuum, largely removed from the reality of how Congress actually functions. An understanding of how Congress operates and how agencies and their respective committees interact reinforces the view that courts, when interpreting statutes, should respect legislators' sense of their own work product. Having set the stage with an examination of the workways of Congress and of agencies, I turn now to a discussion of two differing conceptions—purposivism and textualism—of how courts should interpret statutes and the materials to be used in construing statutes.[15]

Chapter 4

Judicial Interpretation of Statutes

Given my arguments that courts should respect Congress's work product, it will not surprise you that I find authoritative legislative history useful when I interpret statutes. I start with the premise that the role of the courts is to interpret the law in a way that is faithful to its meaning. The role of the court is not to substitute its judgment or to alter the terms of the statute. Judicial respect for Congress and its lawmaking prerogatives in our constitutional scheme requires no less. For a court, that means using the interpretive materials the legislative branch thinks important to understanding its work. Doing so promotes good government as courts applying such methods are more likely to reach results consistent with legislative meaning. Doing so also facilitates healthy interbranch relations as legislators view courts as seeking to hew to the statute's meaning as passed by Congress.

When statutes are unambiguous, as I have noted earlier, the inquiry for a court generally ends with an examination of the words of the statute.[1] At times, even when the statute is plain on its face, the judge may find legislative history helpful in reinforcing the court's understanding of the words. If, for example, the result suggested by the plain language seems absurd, then a broader inquiry, including consideration of legislative history, may be in order. But if that inquiry leads to the same result, then a court cannot alter it, though, as I discuss in subsequent pages, it can bring the perceived interpretive problem to Congress's attention.

Generally, the interpretive problem arises because the statute is ambiguous.[2] From the start, the founders understood that legislation would often be unclear and susceptible to differing interpretations. Madison wrote in *The Federalist* No. 37, describing laws in general:

> All new laws, though penned with the greatest technical skill, and passed on the fullest and most mature deliberation, are considered as more or less obscure and equivocal, until their meaning be liquidated and ascertained by a series of particular discussions and adjudications. Besides the obscurity arising from the complexity of objects, and the imperfection of the human faculties, the medium through which the conceptions of men are conveyed to each other, adds a fresh embarrassment.... [N]o language is so copious as to supply words and phrases for every complex idea, or so correct as not to include many equivocally denoting different ideas. Hence, it must happen that however accurately objects may be discriminated in themselves, and however accurately the discrimination may be considered, the definition of them may be rendered inaccurate by the inaccuracy of the terms in which it is delivered. And this unavoidable inaccuracy must be greater or less, according to the complexity and novelty of the objects defined.[3]

Scholars have long debated what role the founders conceived the judiciary as having—whether it was to be a faithful agent of Congress or a coequal partner with authority to depart from the words of a statute.[4] But how judges were to resolve ambiguities was not something that preoccupied the founders, who were concerned with broad principles of governing and left to Congress whether there would even be federal courts other than the Supreme Court. Although they understood that natural law principles and canons of statutory construction could aid judges, the framers were under no illusion that such tools necessarily dictated particular results.[5] Judges—members of the Supreme Court, other federal judges if Congress authorized them, and state judges—could fill the interpretive void through the exercise of sound judgment. But the framers did not set forth the precise methodology of how judges would do so.[6] It was inevitable, therefore, that as ambiguous statutes were crafted, the question of how to interpret them would become important.

It seems to me that the fundamental task for the judge is to determine what Congress was trying to do in passing the law. In other words, the task is to interpret language in light of the statute's purpose(s) as enacted by legislators, with particular attention to those legislative materials that reliably contribute to understanding the statute's meaning.[7]

A. THE PURPOSIVE APPROACH

The dominant mode of statutory interpretation over the past century has been one premised on the view that legislation is a purposive act, and judges should construe statutes to execute that legislative purpose. This approach finds lineage in the sixteenth-century English decision *Heydon's Case*, which summons judges to interpret statutes in a way "as shall suppress the mischief, and advance the remedy."[8] From this perspective, legislation is the product of a deliberative and informed process. Statutes in this conception have purposes or objectives that are discernible. The task of the judge is to make sense of legislation in a way that is faithful to Congress's purposes. When the text is ambiguous, a court is to provide the meaning that the legislature intended. In that circumstance, the judge gleans the purpose and policy underlying the legislation and deduces the outcome most consistent with those purposes.

The classic exemplar of this approach is found in the 1892 Supreme Court case of *Church of the Holy Trinity v. United States*.[9] The statute in question, the Alien Contract Labor Act, made it unlawful to "prepay the transportation, or in any way assist or encourage the importation or migration of any alien or aliens, any foreigner or foreigners, into the United States...to perform labor or service of any kind."[10] In arranging for an English minister to come to New York to serve as its rector and pastor, the Church of the Holy Trinity seemingly violated the explicit language of the statutory prohibition. But the Court, in an opinion by Justice David Brewer, held that Congress sought to bar only manual labor, not professional services: "[A] thing may be within the letter of the statute and yet not within the statute, because not within its spirit, nor within the intention of its makers."[11] In reaching its conclusion that the law did not apply to the minister's services, the Court went beyond the text of the statute to inquire into underlying purposes. Thus, the Court determined that the statute's title made reference to "labor," not professionals, and that the law was meant to remedy the problem of "great numbers of an ignorant and servile class of foreign laborers."[12] The Court looked to legislative history—to committee hearings, to the House report, which referred to workers "from the lowest social stratum," and to the Senate Labor Committee report, which, in the Court's view, showed that the bill was intended to apply only to manual labor.[13] It also reasoned that because of the role of religion in this country—"this is a Christian nation,"[14] wrote Justice Brewer—Congress could not have intended to make the hiring of a cleric unlawful. With its inquiry beyond the text into the underlying purposes of the statute and with resort to legislative history,[15] *Holy Trinity* became the paradigmatic example of how federal courts in the twentieth century interpreted legislation.[16] It would also, in the view of its critics, such as Justice Scalia, become a prime example of supposed deficiencies in the purposive approach.[17]

Justice Brewer's reasoning in *Holy Trinity* is not unique to his era. Judge Learned Hand of the U.S. Court of Appeals for the Second Circuit echoed *Holy Trinity*:

> All [legislators] have done is to write down certain words which they mean to apply generally to situations of that kind. To apply these literally may either pervert what was plainly their general meaning, or leave undisposed of what there is every reason to suppose they meant to provide for. Thus it is not enough for the judge just to use a dictionary. If he should do no more, he might come out with a result which every sensible man would recognize to be quite the opposite of what was really intended; which would contradict or leave unfulfilled its plain purpose.[18]

The champions of the purposive approach, post–World War II, were two Harvard Law School professors, Henry M. Hart, Jr. and Albert M. Sacks, whose compilations of materials on the legal process influenced generations of jurists and scholars.[19] They wrote that a court's role is to interpret the statutes "to carry out the purpose as best it can," subject to the caveat that it does not give the words either "a meaning they will not bear, or . . . a meaning which would violate any established policy of clear statement."[20] In contrast to the legal realists of the 1930s, who believed that judges make law, the proponents of the legal process approach viewed judges as agents of the legislature with the ability to discern Congress's purposes and to interpret laws consistent with those purposes. Although the canons of construction can be "useful as reassurances about the meaning which particular configurations of words *may* have in an appropriate context," they should not be treated as rigid rules that dictate what these configurations "invariably *must* have" regardless of context.[21] This approach allows for an examination of legislative history so as to better understand the legislation under review. There is much to be said for the view that appreciating the underlying purposes of the legislation allows judges to apply the laws in situations not necessarily anticipated by the enacting Congress. I agree with Justice Breyer, himself a former chief counsel of the Senate Judiciary Committee, that, if courts are faithful to a statute's objectives, Congress, the representative of the people, will view the third branch as a cooperating partner—a perspective that can only promote the fair and effective administration of justice.[22]

Critics of the purposive approach argue that because the laws of Congress are often ambiguous, it is not possible to say with any certainty what the purposes of the legislature are. There may be many purposes, with ambiguity permitting legislators of differing views to vote for a bill, each interpreting it in ways to support their differing conceptions. In the words of Kenneth Shepsle, "Congress [i]s a '[t]hey,' [of 535 legislators] [n]ot an '[i]t,'" and legislative intent is an oxymoron.[23] Legislation—particularly large omnibus bills passed with great speed at the end of a legislative session—may at points be contradictory. As to these large omnibus measures that contain a hodgepodge of unrelated measures, a legislator may vote for the whole bill because she supports certain parts, even though she would vote against other parts if considered separately. In these circumstances, critics of the purposive approach contend that it blinks reality to assert that legislation has knowable purposes that courts can identify.

That legislation is the institutional product of a collection of individuals with a variety of motives and perspectives should not foreclose the effort to discern purposes. Just as intentions are attributed to other large entities—such as local governments, trade associations, and businesses—so too do linguistic protocols, everyday mores, and context facilitate an inquiry into what Congress intended to do when statutory text is vague or ambiguous. At times, it is difficult to ascertain purposes, and the search for purpose as to particular statutes may be elusive. But to jettison the inquiry altogether, because of the difficulty in particular cases, means that judges will interpret statutes unmoored from the reality of the legislative process and what the legislators were seeking to do.

B. THE USES OF LEGISLATIVE HISTORY

I have found legislative history to be helpful in a number of cases on which I have worked on the Second Circuit, including some I discuss in the next chapter. It can aid in the search for meaning when a statute is silent or unclear about a contested issue. Legislative history can be especially valuable when construing a specialized term or phrase in statutes dealing with complex matters beyond the ordinary ken of the judge. In that circumstance, it can aid the judge in understanding how the legislation's congressional proponents wanted the statute to work, what problems they sought to address, what purposes they sought to achieve, and what methods they employed to secure those purposes.[24] Legislative history can be helpful, Justice John Paul Stevens commented, "when an exclusive focus on text seems to convey an incoherent message, but other reliable evidence clarifies the statute and avoids the apparent incoherence."[25] And, at times, as I indicated earlier, authoritative legislative history can be useful, even when the meaning can be discerned from the statute's language, to reinforce or to confirm a court's sense of the text.[26]

When courts construe statutes in ways that respect what legislators consider their work product, the judiciary not only is more likely to reach the correct result, but also promotes comity with the first branch of government. It is a bipartisan institutional perspective within Congress that courts should consider reliable legislative history and that failing to do so impugns Congress's workways. Several years ago, then-Congressman Robert W. Kastenmeier (D-WI), the longtime chair of the House Judiciary Subcommittee on Courts, put it this way: Disregarding legislative history "is an assault on the integrity of the legislative process."[27] Senators Orrin Hatch (R-UT) and Charles E. Grassley (R-IA) as Republican chairs or ranking members of the Judiciary Committee, and Senator Patrick Leahy (D-VT), as Democratic chair or ranking member, have consistently supported judicial resort to legislative history, as did the late Arlen Specter (as R-PA) and then-Senator Joseph R. Biden, Jr. (D-DE). Indeed, senators often press that view on judicial nominees at confirmation hearings.

Senator Grassley, currently ranking member of the Judiciary Committee, has long defended legislative history. In 1986, at the confirmation hearing of Antonin Scalia for Supreme Court Justice, he expressed concern about the then–D.C. Circuit judge's "pretty doggone strong language" in his opposition to legislative history: "[A]s one who has served in Congress for 12 years, legislative history is very important to those of us here who want further detailed expression of that legislative intent."[28] Nearly two decades later, Senator Grassley pressed nominee John G. Roberts, Jr., with a series of questions about legislative history, noting:

> Justice Scalia is of the opinion that most expressions of legislative history, like Committee reports or statements by the Senators on the floor, or in the House, are not entitled to great

weight because they are unreliable indicators of legislative intent. Presumably, Justice Scalia believes that if the members don't actually write a report or don't actually vote on a report, then there is no need to defer to this expression of congressional intent.

Now, obviously, I have great regard for Justice Scalia, his intellect and legal reasoning. But, of course, as I told you in my office, I don't really agree with his position.[29]

Senator Hatch, who for many years was chair or ranking member of the Senate Judiciary Committee, commented that "[t]ext without context often invites confusion and judicial adventurism."[30] As an example of how legislative history might be useful, he pointed to a bail law that did not incorporate a reference to the Speedy Trial Act, but where "[t]he legislative history...imparted the additional information necessary to preserve the basic goal of pretrial detention."[31] Then-Senator Specter of Pennsylvania stated: "I think when justices disregard that kind of material [legislative history], it is just another way to write their own law...."[32]

Consistent with the views of their principals, legislative staffers attest to the importance of legislative history. A central finding of the recent study by Abbe R. Gluck and Lisa Schultz Bressman—the most comprehensive examination of the perspectives of legislative staffs about statutory interpretation ever undertaken—is that "legislative history was emphatically viewed by almost all of our respondents—Republicans and Democrats, majority and minority, alike—as the *most important* drafting and interpretive tool apart from text."[33] The study found that members and their staffs in fact focus more on legislative history than on text when considering and voting on bills; indeed, they often do not read the text of a bill or do not read it closely, but rather pay more attention to the legislative history to understand the bill's purposes and the meaning of particular statutory phrases. Moreover, the survey confirmed that within Congress, committee-crafted legislative history is not viewed as an improper delegation of responsibility to staff, as staffers who draft the legislative history are closely tied to the members for whom they work. Gluck and Bressman also confirmed empirically that legislative history has a wide variety of purposes and audiences beyond courts. It is, as I explained earlier, a tool of congressional oversight of agencies. It is a means of intra-congressional communication to explain in ordinary terms what the bill does, and to provide institutional memory when staffers amend older legislation. Legislative history is also a means of communicating to interested groups and the public. And it is a vehicle for details that drafters think are inappropriate for statutory text because of the sense that too much detail does not belong in the text.[34]

If judges exclude legislative history they will eliminate a useful source of information about the law's meaning. Legislative history is not the law, but can help us understand what the law means. Depriving judges of what appeared to animate legislators risks having courts interpret the legislation in ways that the legislators did not intend, replacing reasoned analysis of what Congress was trying to do with subjective preferences. The danger, as Justice Breyer observed, is that a court will "divorce[] law from life."[35] Those who maintain that it is difficult to discern the purposes of 535 legislators should welcome the use of legislative history; eliminating authoritative materials such as committee reports and conference committee reports as interpretive tools—which can provide valuable guides in understanding purpose—make the interpretive task not only that much harder, but also more prone to incorrect outcomes. Earlier, I explained how those who deal most frequently with statutes—that is, agencies—look to legislative history so as to be faithful to

Congress's meaning. Courts should be no different in examining pre-enactment legislative sources that assist the interpretive task.

C. THE TEXTUALIST CRITIQUE

The approach I advocate has not gone unchallenged. Indeed, within the judiciary, a sustained attack on the use of legislative history began in the 1980s, largely led by Antonin Scalia, first as a D.C. Circuit judge and then as a Supreme Court justice. In a 1993 Supreme Court concurring opinion, he wrote: "We are governed by laws, not by the intentions of legislators.... 'The law as it passed is the will of the majority of both houses, and the only mode in which that will is spoken is in the act itself....'"[36] Justice Scalia is of the view that because legislation often consists of a brew of deals, compromises, and inconsistencies, the search for coherent purpose is elusive. Thus, it is the statute's final wording that must prevail, he has argued, over "unenacted legislative intent."[37] Textualism, as Justice Scalia has championed it, involves an assault on the dependence on any extratextual source in determining statutory meaning. Legislative history became a central target. "We are a Government of laws, not of committee reports," he asserted.[38] In another case, he explained:

> I am confident that only a small proportion of the Members of Congress read either one of the Committee Reports in question...[and] that very few of those who did read them set off for the nearest law library to check out what was actually said in the four cases at issue (or in the more than 50 other cases cited by the House and Senate Reports).... As anyone familiar with modern-day drafting of congressional committee reports is well aware, the

references to the cases were inserted, at best by a committee staff member on his or her own initiative, and at worst by a committee staff member at the suggestion of a lawyer-lobbyist; and the purpose of those references was not primarily to inform the Members of Congress what the bill meant... but rather to influence judicial construction. What a heady feeling it must be for a young staffer, to know that his or her citation of obscure district court cases can transform them into the law of the land, thereafter dutifully to be observed by the Supreme Court itself.[39]

This textualist critique of legislative history has at least four parts. The first, which is premised on the Constitution, is the idea that the only legitimate law is text that both chambers and the President have approved (or passed by a two-thirds vote of Congress over the President's veto). This view looks in part for support from *INS v. Chadha*. In that case, the Supreme Court held legislative vetoes unconstitutional because they evaded procedures of bicameralism, whereby a bill cannot become law without both House and Senate approval, and presentment, whereby all bills that make it through Congress have to be presented to the President for his signature. This emphasis on the twin requirements of bicameralism and presentment is part of the textualist critique. Because (so the narrative goes) legislators do not review legislative history, that history lacks authority. Legislative history materials, Justice Scalia stated, are "frail substitutes for bicameral vote upon the text of a law and its presentment to the President. It is at best dangerous to assume that all the necessary participants in the law-enactment process are acting upon the same unexpressed assumptions."[40] A system that relies on committee reports delegates power to unelected, uncontrolled staff at the expense of the whole chamber, so textualists claim.[41] The use of legislative history, the argument continues, violates the constitutional rule prohibiting congressional self-delegation—the idea that Congress cannot delegate its lawmaking authority to its committees as its agent.[42] Committee reports should not be looked to when interpreting the statute, and neither should materials such as floor debates and statements in the Congressional Record. In the view of legislative history critics, apart from the fact that statements in the Congressional Record are not the laws themselves, the Congressional Record is suspect as a guide to legislative meaning because it does not differentiate between remarks made by those who were involved in crafting the legislation—such as bill managers—and those who were not; it can include statements inserted by legislators who were not present on the floor; and legislators can revise for publication statements that colleagues heard them make on the floor.

Second, critics of legislative history argue that its use impermissibly increases the discretion of judges to roam through the wide range of often inconsistent materials and rely on those that suit their position.[43] By so choosing, critics charge, judges substitute their policy preferences for those of elected officials, with whom such a choice properly resides.

A third component of the assault on legislative history is grounded in the idea that legislators will be compelled to write statutes with more precision if they know that courts cannot consult such materials.

Fourth, underlying the criticism of legislative history is a decidedly negative conception of the legislative process, based on the "public choice" school, which employs principles of market economics to explain decisionmaking.[44] Like many schools, its scholars are not all of one mind and cannot be simply characterized.[45] Generally, though, the public choice school characterizes the legislative process as fueled by rational, egoistic, utility-maximizing legislators whose primary objective is to be re-elected. From this perspective, legislators enact laws that tend, at the expense of the public good and efficiency, to transfer wealth to special interest groups that lobby the legislature. Evading responsibility—so the narrative continues—members of Congress pass unclear statutes, leaving it to administrators and courts to resolve unsettled issues.[46] Laws benefiting society will be few and far between because of the collective action problem. As Mancur Olson put it, "rational, self-interested individuals will not act to achieve their common...interests"[47] by lobbying for legislation that benefits the general public because the benefits being sought are collective to the group as a whole; thus the rational individual is content to be a free rider. In this view, echoing in part Madison's concern in *The Federalist* No. 10, interest groups are unlikely to arise and press legislators to enact "public interest" legislation.

Sharply different from the "public interest" conception, this vision of the legislature is grim.[48] On this conception, legislators—motivated by the goal of reelection—evade choices on critical issues that could provoke opposition from well-organized groups. They do not develop well-conceived legislation, preferring instead to satisfy interest groups through ad hoc bargaining. This view is manifested in Justice Scalia's lament about committee report language written by lawyer-lobbyists at the behest of client groups, and about committees that serve client interests rather than Congress itself, using committee reports to memorialize transactions about which the whole Congress is not aware.[49]

Over time, the textualist critique has become more nuanced. John Manning, who has contributed many distinguished writings in the field, observed that textualists have focused more on formal constitutional arguments such as bicameralism, presentment, and nondelegation. While they continue to look askance at legislative history, they are less inclined to draw upon public choice theory. Rather, they emphasize the importance of judges' "respect[ing] the terms of an enacted text *when its semantic meaning is clear, even if it seems contrary to the statute's apparent overall purpose.*"[50] They take as given the bargaining in the legislative process— whatever the motivations of legislators—and argue that adherence to text is appropriate in part because of legislative compromises, which may make the search for coherent purpose a fool's errand. In interpreting statutes, textualists seek to understand language in a linguistic context, looking to dictionary definitions,[51] colloquial meanings, the technical definitions of terms of art, and background conventions associated with certain phrases or types of legislation.[52]

Although I agree that dictionaries can be helpful—especially when dealing with a specialized term, or a term of art, or a word's usage at the time of the law's enactment—more often than not, the interpretive challenge comes from the ambiguity of the word as situated in a sentence. In that situation, dictionaries can hardly be definitive. In any event, if it is appropriate to look to a dictionary as an extraneous source, it is not at all clear why legislative history—in its reliable forms—should be excluded. More fundamentally, congressional drafting practices suggest caution with regard to excessive reliance on dictionaries: The Gluck-Bressman survey of legislative staff indicated that although they were cognizant of the judicial trend, "[m]ore than 50% of our respondents said that dictionaries are never or rarely used when drafting."[53] Legislative drafters often create their own definitional sections in statutes. Yet, as James Brudney and Lawrence Baum have observed, dictionary definitions may trump statutory definitions in Supreme Court opinions.[54] Indeed, they argue there is more cherry-picking of dictionary sources than of legislative history in those opinions.[55]

D. TEXTUALISTS' IMPACT

There is a substantial literature, to which I have offered some writings, that questions the underlying factual assertions for textualists' sweeping propositions.[56] That textualists have moved away from public choice theory is understandable, given the inability of that theory to capture the complexity of the decisionmaking process. The calculus of Congress cannot be reduced only to the idea that interest groups dictate the behavior, votes, and agenda of legislators eager for the financial support necessary for reelection.[57] A variety of case studies track the passage of legislation where interest group involvement was not decisive.[58] And where groups have had a role, their interests, as James Q. Wilson has written, have not necessarily been economic.[59] Moreover, some legislation predated interest groups' activity and, indeed, led to the creation of particular interest groups. One example is section 504 of the Rehabilitation Act of 1973, outlawing discrimination against those with disabilities in programs receiving federal aid or assistance—a measure that was not the product of interest group activity, but after whose passage existing groups increased their efforts and new groups were born.[60] And certainly, in spite of the opposition of large powerful economic interests, Congress has enacted a variety of legislation. Examples include laws having to do with airline and trucking deregulation and measures addressing health, environmental, and safety concerns.[61]

Surely, legislators are concerned about reelection,[62] and public choice theory quite usefully draws attention to how incentives can affect behavior. It would be naive to think that legislators do not consider how interest groups can affect, positively or negatively, their hopes to return to office. But legislators also have policy objectives that cannot simply be understood as interest group driven. Even where interest groups have a substantial impact on the legislative process, it does not follow that their goals are against the public interest.[63] Legislation that benefits the personal interests of an interest group may, depending on the measure, also benefit the wider public.

Textualists have appropriately identified misuses and manipulation of legislative history. Without doubt, language is on occasion put into committee reports unnoticed by the whole legislative chamber or even by members of relevant committees. Martin D. Ginsburg, for example, pointed to such excesses in the area of tax legislation,[64] and Senator Moynihan once expressed concern that report language in one particular piece of legislation was not reviewed by the legislators on the relevant committee.[65] By putting a spotlight on legislative history, the textualist critique has had some effect on individual legislators. Then-Representative Barney Frank (D-MA) reportedly warded off an effort to insert compromise language in a committee report rather than in the bill itself.[66] He did so with two words: "Justice Scalia."[67] Although pure textualists can claim among Supreme Court Justices only Antonin Scalia and Clarence Thomas as faithful supporters,[68] the textualist critique has had an undeniable impact. Today, it is commonplace for a statutory opinion of a federal court to state: "where the statutory language provides a clear answer, it [statutory interpretation] ends there as well."[69]

Gone are the days when a Supreme Court would declare, as it did in 1971:

> The legislative history of both § 4(f) of the Department of Transportation Act, 49 U.S.C. § 1653(f) (1964 ed., Supp. V), and § 138 of the Federal-Aid Highway Act, 23 U.S.C. § 138 (1964 ed., Supp. V), is ambiguous.... Because of this ambiguity, it is clear that we must look primarily to the statutes themselves to find the legislative intent.[70]

By 2005, Justice Anthony Kennedy, in an opinion of the Court, to which Justices Stevens, Sandra Day O'Connor, Ginsburg, and Breyer dissented, would exclaim:

> Extrinsic materials have a role in statutory interpretation only to the extent they shed a reliable light on the enacting Legislature's understanding of otherwise ambiguous terms. Not all extrinsic materials are reliable sources of insight into legislative understandings...and legislative history in particular is vulnerable to two serious criticisms. First, [it is] often murky, ambiguous, and contradictory.... [It often becomes, in] Judge Leventhal's memorable phrase, an exercise in "looking over a crowd and picking out your friends."... Second, judicial reliance on legislative materials like committee reports, which are not themselves subject to the requirements of Article I, may give unrepresentative committee members—or, worse yet, unelected staffers and lobbyists—both the power and the incentive to attempt strategic manipulations of legislative history to secure results they were unable to achieve through the statutory text.[71]

While judges still use legislative history,[72] they tend to give it more of a supporting rather than a leading role in statutory interpretation.[73] In one such case, Justice Sotomayor stated that "although we need not rely on legislative history given the text's clarity, we note that the history only supports our interpretation of 'individual' [the statutory term at issue]."[74] In another, Justice Kagan, writing for a unanimous court, began by focusing on the text, whose "clarity" could "end" the Court's consideration; looked next at the context of the statute to "put[] an exclamation point on this textual conclusion"; and only then assessed legislative history. As she wrote: "Finally, for those who consider legislative history useful, the key Senate Report... provides one last piece of corroborating evidence."[75] Courts tend to approach legislative history with what Justice Ginsburg termed "hopeful skepticism."[76]

E. A CRITIQUE OF TEXTUALISM

Although textualists have helpfully shown some of the pitfalls of legislative history, they have not made the case for its exclusion. I question their view that restricting interpretation to the text will lead to more responsible legislating and more clearly drafted laws. Certainly, textual ambiguity may be a consequence of carelessly drafted laws. And sometimes rather than confront difficult problems in text, legislative drafters may address them in committee reports. But ambiguity is often the product of the simple fact that the issues are difficult and Congress, having identified the general problem, leaves it to an agency or court to determine how best to address the problem in its specifics.[77] As Richard Stewart observed: "The demands on Congress's agenda far exceed its capacity to make collective decisions."[78] Given policy complexities, it is unreasonable to expect Congress to anticipate all interpretive questions that may present themselves in the future.[79] Inadvertence as a result of time pressures may be the explanation, especially when rapidly drafted amendments are added to larger bills. In other circumstances, it may be that the sponsors were unable or deliberately chose not to craft legislation that was both precise and enactable. The language may be imprecise in order to facilitate the bill's passage, such that even competing interests can find language in the bill that supports their positions. Ambiguity, as Herbert Kaufman remarked, can be the solvent of disagreement, at least temporarily.[80] In these circumstances, textualists should be under no illusions that decrying ambiguity will change legislative behavior.[81]

As to constraining judicial preferences, it seems to me that excluding legislative history when interpreting ambiguous statutes is just as likely to expand a judge's discretion as reduce it. When a statute is unambiguous, resorting to legislative history is generally not necessary; in that circumstance, the inquiry ordinarily ends. But when a statute is ambiguous, barring legislative history leaves a judge only with words that could be interpreted in a variety of ways without contextual guidance as to what legislators may have thought. Lacking such guidance increases the probability that a judge will construe a law in a manner that the legislators did not intend. It is seemingly inconsistent that textualists, who look to such extratextual materials as the records of the Constitutional Convention and *The Federalist* in interpreting the Constitution, would look askance at the use of legislative history sources when interpreting legislation. As scholars have pointed out, the records of the Constitutional Convention consulted by textualists are themselves incomplete.[82]

The contention that the use of legislative history violates the constitutional proscription against self-delegation—whereby Congress purportedly cedes lawmaking authority to its committees—is premised on a mistaken view of the legislative process. Legislative history accompanying proposed legislation precedes legislative enactment. When Congress passes a law, it can be said to incorporate the materials that it, or at least the law's principal sponsors (and others who worked to secure enactment), deem useful in interpreting the law.[83] After all, Article I of the Constitution gives each chamber the authority to set its own procedures for the introduction, consideration, and approval of bills. And each chamber has established its own rules and practices[84] governing lawmaking—some favoring certain proceedings over others—establishing "a resultant hierarchy of internal communications."[85] Those rules and procedures give particular legislators, such as committee chairs, floor managers, and party leaders, substantial control over the process by which legislation is enacted. Communications from such members as to the meaning of proposed statutes can provide reliable signals to the whole chamber. And, as I noted earlier, members and their staffs, who well understand that maintaining credibility with colleagues is essential to effective legislating, have every incentive to represent accurately the meaning of proposed statutes to colleagues, as written and discussed in legislative history. For their part, legislative staffers, who serve at the pleasure of the members, generally seek to serve their principals as faithful agents; they well recognize that their tenure will be short-lived if they undertake actions that do not reflect what their principals want, or pursue agendas independent of or contrary to those of their principals.[86]

The paucity of judicial knowledge about congressional rules and processes relating to the legislative process, as Victoria Nourse has commented, is striking; that lack of knowledge can impede the judiciary's efforts to interpret statutes.[87] As she writes: "If nothing else, as a matter of legislative supremacy, if courts must respect Congress's decisions, then judges—and administrators, where it may matter more—must begin the process of understanding Congress's methods."[88] The empirical findings of the Gluck-Bressman study[89] that in Congress legislative history is the most important drafting and interpretive instrument apart from text, that members and staffs rely more on legislative history than the text of bills, that the committee system is not an improper delegation of authority, that dictionaries are not often used, and that canons are of limited utility all suggest quite powerfully this conclusion: when courts fail to appreciate the dynamics of the legislative process, they undermine their capacity to reach sound judicial decisions as to legislative meaning.

F. CANONS OF STATUTORY CONSTRUCTION

In their impressive book, *Reading Law: The Interpretation of Legal Texts,* Justice Scalia and his coauthor, Professor Bryan Garner, reject legislative history and urge a renewed focus on canons of statutory construction.[90] Canons, after all, have long been looked to by courts to provide stable rules of construction. Many have existed across centuries, while others have developed more recently. The canons include such precepts as:

- every word of a statute must be given significance;
- repeals by implication are disfavored (a statute will not be considered as repealing prior acts on the same subject in the absence of express words to that effect, unless there is an irreconcilable repugnancy between them, or unless the new law is evidently intended to supersede all prior acts);
- the expression of one thing is the exclusion of another;
- penal statutes are to be interpreted narrowly;
- if the language is plain, construction is unnecessary;
- the starting point is the language of the statute;
- when a list of two or more descriptors is followed by more general descriptors, the otherwise wide meaning of the general descriptors must be restricted to the same class, if any, of the specific words that precede them.

Justice Scalia and Professor Garner argue that what they term "valid canons" of construction lead to more constrained and predictable judicial decisions. They identify thirty-seven sound principles of interpretation applicable to all texts, including such fundamental principles as "the words of a governing text are of paramount concern, and what they convey, in their text, is what the text means";[91] semantic canons such as "words are to be understood in their ordinary, everyday meanings—unless the context indicates that they bear a technical sense"; syntactic canons such as "words are to be given the meaning that the proper grammar and usage would assign them"; and contextual canons such as the absurdity doctrine that "a provision may be either disregarded or judicially corrected as an error (when the correction is textually simple) if failing to do so would result in a disposition that no reasonable person could approve."[92]

Justice Scalia and Professor Garner set forth twenty principles applicable specifically to governmental prescriptions. They include: "expected meaning canons," for instance, "the constitutional-doubt canon" that a statute should be interpreted in a way that avoids placing its constitutionality in doubt;[93] "government-structuring canons," which include so-called clear statement canons, such as the precept that a statute does not waive sovereign immunity—and a federal statute does not eliminate state sovereign immunity—unless that disposition is unequivocally clear, and the canon that a federal statute is presumed to supplement rather than displace state law;[94] and "private-right canons," such as the rule of lenity, whereby ambiguity in a statute defining a crime or imposing a penalty should be resolved in the defendant's favor.[95] They also discuss thirteen "falsities"; for example, they view as false the notion that committee reports and floor speeches are worthwhile aids in statutory construction.[96]

The usefulness of canons has long been debated. Karl N. Llewllleyn argued in his classic work of more than six decades ago that for virtually every canon there is an equal and opposite canon that can be invoked to justify any decision.[97] This view has met with criticism,[98] and indeed I have found that universally accepted canons can be useful.[99] At the same time, canons have their limits as guides to adjudication. Judge Richard A. Posner put it this way:

"[T]here is no canon for ranking or choosing between canons; the code lacks a key."[100] Justice Scalia and Professor Garner forthrightly acknowledge: "No canon of interpretation is absolute. Each may be overcome by the strength of differing principles that point in other directions."[101] Take, for example, the absurdity doctrine and the principle that texts should be interpreted as the words indicate, no matter what. The idea that a judge should be faithful to text no matter where it leads is seemingly at odds with the application of the absurdity doctrine. The application of the absurdity doctrine enlarges judicial discretion rather than constrains it, and that exercise of discretion seems at war with the textualist view that the use of canons will limit judicial choices.[102]

More fundamentally, wiping out legislative history, in the face of empirical evidence that Congress views it as essential in understanding its meaning, leaves us largely with a canon-based interpretive regime that may not only fail to reflect the reality of the legislative process, but may also undermine the constitutional understanding that Congress's statutemaking should be respected as a democratic principle. Certainly, it is safe to assume that most legislators do not know that canons even exist—most legislators are not lawyers, and most lawyers are not trained in legislative drafting. Many years ago, former Congressman, and later judge, Abner J. Mikva observed: "[T]he only 'canons' we talked about were the ones the Pentagon bought that could not shoot straight."[103] And we would expect that while the staffs of the offices of legislative counsel may be familiar with the canons, understanding of the canons will more likely be uneven across committees, with the judiciary committees having the most knowledge. The comprehensive Gluck-Bressman study conclusively shows that congressional staffers are familiar with some canons and not others, and reject some canons of which they are aware. For example, while drafters cannot generally identify by name the legal canon "noscitur a sociis"(ambiguous terms in a list are to be construed in reference to other terms on the list), they overwhelmingly accept that concept in drafting legislation.[104] But the study found that most respondents are not cognizant of and do not use "clear statement rules" (requiring statutory text to be unambiguous if it is to overcome canonical presumptions in particular areas of policy); do not use dictionaries; and view legislative history as a critical tool.[105]

Whether or not Congress is aware of the canons, the courts can use them in ways that fundamentally shape outcomes differently than how Congress intended, as when courts impose clear statement canons. If legislative drafters are not cognizant of the clear statement rules, they risk writing legislation that faces court challenges that they could not have anticipated. Then, if Congress disagrees with the court's decision, it will have to determine whether to overturn the court ruling with a new statute that in some way restores the legislative outcome that it had previously enacted.

It is, at least on first blush, appealing to think that canons could be crafted reflecting universal agreement in Congress, courts, and agencies.[106] But in the absence of such an understanding, in many cases the canons can be helpful only up to a point. Even if one were to arrive at shared conventions, it is problematic to interpret statutes, passed against the backdrop of then-existing judicial doctrines, in light of newly created canons. As Stephen Breyer, then the chief judge of the U.S. Court of Appeals for the First Circuit, wrote: "To change horses in midstream, suddenly to ignore a statute's history when those who directly or indirectly helped to enact it expected the contrary, would defeat their expectations and, in a sense (if the change were sufficiently sudden and radical), those of the voters as well."[107]

At the end of the day, we are left with the ineluctable conclusion that whatever the value of canons, the value of legislative history cannot be denied as an important indicator of legislative meaning, and that a court should be mindful of the preferences of the elected legislature.

G. CONCLUDING THOUGHTS

Chief Justice John Roberts, who makes use of legislative history, stated at his confirmation hearing that "[a]ll legislative history is not created equal. There's a difference between the weight that you give a conference report and the weight you give a statement of one legislator on the floor. You have to, I think, have some degree of sensitivity in understanding exactly what you're looking at...."[108] I concur. The task, as Senator Hatch commented, is to draw upon legislative history "properly applied" in "reliable forms,"[109] and to separate the wheat from the chaff among legislative materials. For courts, that means, in part, having a better understanding of the legislative process and its rules,[110] and appreciating the internal hierarchy of communications. Conference committee reports and committee reports should sit at the top of authority, followed by statements of the bill's managers in the Congressional Record, with stray statements of legislators on the floor—who had heretofore not been involved in consideration of the bill—at the bottom. To explain how I, as a judge, try to discern legislative meaning, drawing upon the materials of the legislative process, I focus in the next chapter on three cases in which I was the writing judge.

Chapter 5

Some Cases I Have Decided

Most judges, in my experience, are neither wholly textualists nor wholly purposivists (that is, seekers of purpose). Purposivists tend not to go beyond the words of an unambiguous statute; at times, textualists look to purposes and extratextual sources such as dictionaries. What sets the two apart is a difference in emphasis and the tools they employ to find meaning.

In approaching the interpretive task, a judge can use several tools, including: text, statutory structure, history, word usage in other relevant statutes, common law usages, agency interpretations, dictionary definitions, technical and scientific usages, lay usages, canons, common practices, and purpose.[1] The judge's work takes place not on the lofty plane of grand, unified theory, but on the ground of practical, common-sense inquiry.[2] The judge pulls from the toolbox those instruments that can help extract "[u]seful [k]nowledge,"[3] as Benjamin Franklin termed it, about what the statute means in light of congressional purposes. For example, the toolbox can help the judge appreciate the institutional context that may serve as a guide to understanding a statute's meaning. Statutes vary in design and substance,[4] and so the interpretive task may change and the tools used may vary depending on the particular statutory issue at hand.

As I have noted, some statutes are precise, specific, and closed-ended, such that the text itself provides definitive direction. For such statutes, as Justice David Souter said, "[t]he language is straight-forward, and with a straightforward application ready to hand, stat-utory interpretation has no business getting metaphysical."[5] I have had many cases where resort to the text was all that I needed to re-solve the case. Two examples suffice. In a case to which I alluded in the introduction, I had to interpret these words: "It shall be unlawful for any person to knowingly or intentionally purchase at retail dur-ing a 30 day period more than 9 grams of…pseudoephedrine base…in a scheduled listed chemical product…."[6] The appellant (the person appealing the district court decision) had been con-victed of purchasing 24.48 grams in a thirty-day period. Under the plain words of the statute, he unquestionably violated the law.[7] In another case, I had to construe a section of a statute requiring proof that a defendant engaged in obstructive conduct "with the intent to impede, obstruct, or influence the investigation or proper adminis-tration *of any matter within the jurisdiction of any department or agency of the United States*."[8] The appellants asserted that the govern-ment was obligated to link their conduct with knowledge of a pend-ing or imminent official proceeding at the time the statement was given and an intention to affect that proceeding. But the section at issue makes no specific reference to official proceeding. The appel-lants' argument thus conflicted with the plain meaning of the statute. As my panel said: "The words of the statute are unambiguous, and, thus, 'judicial inquiry is complete.'"[9]

Some statutes deal with subjects where words have specialized meanings. Tax law is an example, as its subtleties are not necessarily obvious in the text itself. Still other statutes are more open-ended in construction, such that agencies and courts must go beyond the text in the interpretive process. For instance, it is not self-evident what constitute "unfair methods of competition in or affecting com-merce, and unfair or deceptive acts or practices in or affecting commerce."[10] Nor is it self-evident what constitutes a "reasonable accommodation" under the Americans with Disabilities Act.[11] In deciphering statutes, we would do well to remember Justice Felix Frankfurter's observation: "Unhappily, there is no table of logarithms for statutory construction.... One or another [item of evidence] may be decisive in one set of circumstances, while of little value elsewhere."[12]

To examine more concretely approaches to statutory interpretation, and the challenges of construing statutes, I offer three cases in which I was the writing judge. I've chosen cases where the panel believed that there was a textual ambiguity that needed to be addressed and where the Supreme Court granted review. In two cases, the Supreme Court agreed, and in one the Court disagreed. One case shows the limits of simply relying on text (*Gayle*); the second, the importance of understanding statutory purposes (*Raila*); and the final case, the uses of legislative history (*Murphy*). To give a sense of how the court approached the case at hand, I often draw here directly from, or paraphrase closely, the language of the various judicial opinions I discuss. I leave the reader to reach her own conclusions about whether the courts' decisions were persuasive.

Just a background note: When I consider statutory issues, it is in the context of an appeal from a decision of a federal district court, where cases generally originate in the federal system, and sometimes in the context of an appeal from a ruling of an administrative body, such as the Department of Justice's Board of Immigration Appeals. Whereas a district court decision is the product of one district judge sitting alone, on the Court of Appeals, I decide cases with two other colleagues—the three of us constitute the panel. Judges are assigned to sit on panels, and all cases are assigned randomly to panels. When I have the assignment to write the opinion that explains the panel's decision, I secure valuable input from my colleagues, and the final product reflects collective decisionmaking. Parties dissatisfied with the decision of the Court of Appeals panel may seek review in the Supreme Court, although the Court rarely grants such review.[13]

A. *RAILA V. UNITED STATES*, 355 F.3D 118 (2D CIR. 2004), ENDORSED BY THE SUPREME COURT IN *DOLAN V. UNITED STATES POSTAL SERVICE*, 546 U.S. 481 (2006)

Understanding Statutory Purpose: Whether "negligent transmission" in the postal context refers only to the actual delivery of mail or more broadly to negligent actions occurring in the process of transmission

Raila v. United States is a case in which our panel (Richard Cardamone, Sonia Sotomayor, and I) had to make sense of what we perceived as an ambiguous statute where the legislative history was scant. In a case involving the same statute, the Third Circuit disagreed with our reading, and the Supreme Court agreed to review that case in order to resolve the circuit split. As you will see, the text provided few clues; indeed, under some readings it could have led to absurd results. It was thus necessary to go beyond the text per se to discern the statutory purpose animating the legislation.

Plaintiff Lenore Raila was injured when she slipped on a package that a postal worker had left just below her front door step. She filed suit against the United States under the Federal Tort Claims Act ("FTCA"),[14] alleging that the proximate cause, i.e., the most direct cause, of her injuries was the negligence of the postal employee who placed the package where someone might slip on it. That 1946 statute broadly waived the United States' sovereign immunity, that is, the privilege providing that it cannot be sued, with regard to suits in tort. It conferred jurisdiction on the district courts to hear claims "for injury or loss of property, or personal injury or death caused by the negligent or wrongful act or omission of any employee of the Government while acting within the scope of his office or employment, under circumstances where the United States, if a private person, would be liable to the claimant in accordance with the law of the place where the act or omission occurred."[15] However, Congress carved out certain exceptions to this broad waiver of sovereign immunity. One exception, codified at 28 U.S.C. § 2680(b) (2000), commonly referred to as the "postal matter exception," preserves sovereign immunity for "[a]ny claim arising out of the loss, miscarriage, or negligent transmission of letters or postal matter."[16]

At issue in this case was the meaning of the phrase "negligent transmission." Specifically, the question was whether the word "transmission" applies to the situation in this case, such that the government is immune to suit. The government moved to dismiss the complaint on the ground that the district court lacked subject matter jurisdiction, because the postal matter exception shields the government from liability. The judge on the U.S. District Court for the District of Connecticut who heard the case looked to the ordinary meaning of the statutory language and noted that *Webster's Third New International Dictionary* defines "transmit" as "to cause to go or be conveyed to another person or place." In addition, the judge cited other district court decisions that interpreted the postal matter exception. A district judge in Georgia found that transmission begins "when a postal patron deposits postal matter with the Postal Service and...end[s] when the postal matter [i]s delivered by the Postal Service to a third-party," and thus the exception covered acts of negligence by Postal Service employees up to the point of delivery.[17] And a New Jersey district judge held that the postal matter exception shielded the government from liability for negligent placement of a package that resulted in a slip and fall.[18] For these reasons, the district judge in Connecticut concluded that the government had not waived sovereign immunity in this kind of case and granted the government's motion to dismiss the complaint.

Ms. Raila appealed the judge's decision to the Court of Appeals, and the clerk of court randomly assigned the case to our panel. We unanimously reversed the district judge's decision.

Our panel observed that the Supreme Court had held that, in construing the exceptions to the FTCA's waiver of sovereign immunity, courts should look to the intent of Congress. "[W]e should not take it upon ourselves," the justices wrote, "to extend the waiver beyond that which Congress intended. Neither, however, should we assume the authority to narrow the waiver that Congress intended."[19] The postal matter exception, to reiterate, excludes "[a]ny claim arising out of the loss, miscarriage, or negligent transmission of letters or postal matter." The issue that we had to resolve was whether "negligent transmission" refers only to negligence that results in loss of, or damage to, the postal material itself, or whether "negligent transmission" also encompasses the negligent placement of postal material that causes injury to someone or something other than the mail.

We first noted that statutory construction begins with the plain text, and, "where the statutory language provides a clear answer, it ends there as well."[20] We observed that in evaluating ambiguity we also look to the statutory scheme as a whole and place the particular provision within the context of that statute.[21] To us, the meaning of the words "negligent transmission" was not self-evident. Because a postal worker's every step is, on some level, taken as part of the "transmission of letters [and] postal matter"—that being the business of the Postal Service—the phrase "negligent transmission" could plausibly embrace every negligent act by any postal employee.

In referring to "loss, miscarriage, or negligent transmission," however, we thought it likely that Congress, in keeping with the concept of *noscitur a sociis*—the notion that the meaning of a word may be ascertained by reference to the meaning of the words associated with it—intended "negligent transmission" to be interpreted more narrowly, so as to be consonant with the words "loss" and "miscarriage."[22] The words "loss" and "miscarriage" refer only to damage and delay of the postal material itself and consequential damages therefrom. Interpreted this way, we concluded, the postal matter exception preserves sovereign immunity against claims for such damage, but it permits suits for other injuries, such as those that result from a slip and fall on a package that was left in the wrong place.

We observed that the Supreme Court, in interpreting the postal matter exception, noted that its language is narrower than the language of other exceptions to the FTCA.[23] For example, other statutes preserve sovereign immunity for any claim arising from the activities of the Tennessee Valley Authority[24] and the Panama Canal Company.[25] Another, codified in 28 U.S.C. § 2680(c), bars "[a]ny claim arising in respect of the assessment or collection of any tax or customs duty."[26] However, the postal matter exception does not categorically bar all claims arising from the activities of the Postal Service, but only those arising from the loss, miscarriage, or negligent transmission of letters or postal matter. As the Supreme Court observed in *Kosak v. United States*:

> The specificity of § 2680(b), in contrast with the generality of § 2680(c), suggests, if anything, that Congress intended the former to be *less* encompassing than the latter. The motivation for such an intent is not hard to find. One of the principal purposes of the [FTCA] was to waive the Government's immunity from liability for injuries resulting from auto accidents in which

employees of the Postal System were at fault. In order to ensure that § 2680(b), which governs torts committed by mailmen, did not have the effect of barring precisely the sort of suit that Congress was most concerned to authorize, the draftsmen of the provision carefully delineated the types of misconduct for which the Government was not assuming financial responsibility—namely, "the loss, miscarriage, or negligent transmission of letters or postal matter"—thereby excluding, by implication, negligent handling of motor vehicles.[27]

The government's attorneys did not contest that one of the primary purposes of the FTCA was to waive the sovereign immunity of the United States for accidents caused by the negligence of postal employees driving postal vehicles—and that the postal matter exception was never intended to bar such claims. If that exception does not prevent such claims, as we thought the government correctly asserted, we saw no logical reason to bar claims resulting from the negligence of the postal employee who places a package where someone might slip on it.

We next considered the relatively limited legislative history of the FTCA with respect to the provision at issue. A committee report on a prior version of the legislation noted that "the common-law torts of employees of regulatory agencies would be included within the scope of the bill.... Thus, [the exceptions] ... are not intended to exclude such common-law torts as an automobile collision caused by the negligence of [a government employee]."[28]

At a hearing in 1940 on a previous version of the legislation before a Senate subcommittee, Abraham Holtzoff, a Special Assistant to the Attorney General, testified that "[e]very person who sends a piece of postal matter can protect himself by registering it, as provided by the postal laws and regulations. It would be intolerable, of course, if in any case of loss or delay the Government could be sued for damages. Consequently, this provision was inserted."[29] We believed that this testimony suggested that the purpose of the postal matter exception was to shield the government from liability arising from loss of or harm to the mail itself, not for injuries caused by the common law torts of postal employees. In interpreting the postal matter exception, a district judge—citing the Holtzoff testimony—found that "Congress was concerned with shielding the courts from the potential landslide of lawsuits that might be generated by the unavoidable mishaps incident to the ordinary, accepted operation of delivering millions of packages and letters each year."[30] The judge sensibly concluded that where the nature of the injury was such that the injured party could not protect himself or herself by registering the parcel, the postal matter exception did not apply.

Further, our panel believed that the government's interpretation would lead to absurd results. For example, consider a situation in which a Postal Service employee is driving a postal truck in the course of a mail delivery route. The driver throws a package toward the home to which it is to be delivered. The package hits a pedestrian and causes injury. At the same time, the driver has taken his eye off the road, and the truck strikes another pedestrian, killing him. Under the government's proposed interpretation of "negligent transmission," the government would be liable for the injury caused by the truck, but not by the flying package.

Our panel also considered a situation in which two customers enter a post office and one turns right, the other turns left. Both slip on puddles of water that had been created through the negligence of postal employees. One puddle was created when a postal worker negligently dropped a parcel, shattering a vessel containing liquid. The other puddle was created by the janitor, who failed to wipe away all the water when washing the floor. Under the government's proposed construction of "negligent transmission" the government would be liable for the injury caused by the janitor's puddle, but not for the injury caused by the shattered vessel, because the latter negligence occurred during the "transmission" of postal material. At oral argument, the government agreed that in each of these two hypothetical situations, there would be liability to one plaintiff but not the other. Those results, we believed, are plainly absurd and caution against adoption of the government's interpretation of the statute.

The government's lawyers had told us that rejecting its interpretation could result in a large volume of litigation. We said that we could not predict with any certainty the consequences of our holding. In any event, our task was not to make policy, but rather, constrained by the words of the statute, to interpret its language consistent with the intent of Congress. We pointed out that Congress has the capacity to amend the statute to render the government immune from similar actions and can do so if it wishes. Accordingly, we held that the postal matter exception did not bar Raila's claims and that the district judge erred in dismissing the complaint for lack of subject matter jurisdiction.

The Third Circuit Disagrees: Dolan v. United States Postal Service, 377 F.3d 285 (3d Cir. 2004)

Not long after our panel announced its decision, a panel of the Court of Appeals for the Third Circuit considered the same issue. A postal customer, Barbara Dolan, brought suit against the government under the FTCA seeking to recover for injuries suffered when she tripped over mail negligently left on her porch by a mail carrier. Noting that our decision interpreted "negligent transmission" to be limited to the loss or miscarriage of postal material, the Third Circuit forthrightly stated:

> We disagree with that holding. To the extent that "negligent transmission" is ambiguous at all, any ambiguities in the language of a purported waiver of sovereign immunity must be construed in favor of the government. Construing 2680(b) in such a way is made all the easier by the statute's expansive language. The phrase "[a]ny claim arising out" evinces Congress's intent to broaden rather than limit the exception for "negligent transmission of letters or postal matter." Moreover, § 2680(b)'s legislative history makes plain that Congress intended to protect the government from lawsuits that might be generated by the unavoidable mishaps incident to the ordinary accepted operations of delivering millions of packages and letters each year.[31]

The Supreme Court Resolves the Circuit Split: Dolan v. United States Postal Service, 546 U.S. 481 (2006)

With the Second and Third Circuits in disagreement, the Supreme Court granted a writ of certiorari in *Dolan* and heard the appeal. (The Court is not required to resolve disagreements among courts of appeals, known as "circuit splits," but it will often do so if it believes the issue needs resolution.) The high court sided with our decision, and reversed and remanded the case to the Third Circuit (i.e., sent the case back to the Court of Appeals to reconsider in light of the Supreme Court decision). Justice Kennedy wrote the majority opinion, joined by Chief Justice Roberts, and Justices Stevens, Scalia, Souter, Ginsburg, and Breyer. Justice Thomas filed a dissenting opinion, and Justice Samuel Alito took no part in the case.

The Court assumed that under the applicable state law a person injured by tripping over a package or bundle negligently left by a private party would have a cause of action for damages. The question was whether the postal matter exception preserves sovereign immunity in such a case. The Court acknowledged that "negligent transmission," considered in isolation, could embrace a wide range of negligent acts committed by the Postal Service in the course of delivering mail, including creation of slip-and-fall hazards from leaving packets and parcels on the porch of a residence. "After all," Justice Kennedy wrote, "in ordinary meaning and usage, transmission of the mail is not complete until it arrives at its destination."[32] He referred, for example, to *Webster's Third New International Dictionary*, which defines "transmission" as "an act, process, or instance of transmitting" and "transmit" as "to cause to go or be conveyed to another person or place." In large part, the majority opinion said, this inference—transmission includes delivery—led the district court and court of appeals in the *Dolan* case to rule for the government. However, asserted Justice Kennedy, interpretation of a word or phrase depends upon reading the whole statutory text, considering the statute's purpose and context: here, both context and precedent require reading the phrase so that it does not go beyond negligence that causes mail to be lost or to arrive late, in damaged condition, or at the wrong address.

Starting with context, he wrote that in the statute the term "negligent transmission" follows the terms "loss" and "miscarriage." Those terms, he continued, limit the reach of "transmission." Justice Kennedy looked to the more colloquial version of *noscitur a sociis* when he stated that "'a word is known by the company it keeps'—a rule that 'is often wisely applied where a word is capable of many meanings in order to avoid the giving of unintended breadth to the Acts of Congress.'"[33] Here, Justice Kennedy noted that mail is "lost" if it is destroyed or misplaced and "miscarried" if it goes to the wrong address. Since both terms refer to failings in the postal obligation to deliver mail in a timely manner to the right address, the Court determined that it would be odd if "negligent transmission" swept far more broadly to include injuries caused by postal employees but involving neither failure to transmit mail nor damage to its contents.

This interpretation, the Court found, was also supported by the Court's previous decision in *Kosak*, which noted that one of the FTCA's purposes was to waive the government's immunity from liability for injuries resulting from auto accidents involving postal trucks delivering—and thus "transmitting"—the mail. Nothing in the statutory text, Justice Kennedy commented, supported a distinction between negligent driving, which the government claimed relates only circumstantially to the mail, and Dolan's accident, which was caused by the mail itself. In both cases the postal employee acted negligently while transmitting mail. In addition, the Court majority pointed to my panel's recognition, which the government acknowledged, that focusing on whether the mail itself caused the injury would yield anomalies, perhaps making liability turn on whether a mail sack causing a slip and fall was empty or full, or whether a pedestrian sideswiped by a passing truck was hit by the side-view mirror or a dangling parcel.

It is more likely, Justice Kennedy contended, that Congress intended to retain immunity only for injuries arising because mail either fails to arrive or arrives late, in damaged condition, or at the wrong address, since such harms are primarily identified with the Postal Service's function of transporting mail. The government claimed that, given the Postal Service's vast operations, Congress must have intended to insulate delivery-related torts from liability; however, § 2680(b)'s specificity indicates otherwise. Justice Kennedy said that had Congress intended to preserve immunity for all delivery-related torts, it could have used sweeping language similar to that used in other FTCA exceptions. By instead "carefully delineat[ing]" just three types of harm (loss, miscarriage, and negligent transmission), Congress expressed the intent to immunize only a subset of postal wrongdoing, not all torts committed in the course of mail delivery.[34]

Furthermore, Justice Kennedy argued, losses of the type for which immunity is retained under the postal matter exception are at least to some degree avoidable or compensable through postal registration and insurance. When the government raised the specter of frivolous slip-and-fall claims inundating the Postal Service, Justice Kennedy dismissed this concern as a risk shared by any business making home deliveries. Finally, the Supreme Court majority stated that the general rule that a sovereign immunity waiver "will be strictly construed...in favor of the sovereign"[35] is "unhelpful" in the FTCA context, where "unduly generous interpretations of the exceptions run the risk of defeating the central purpose of the statute," which "waives the Government's immunity from suit in sweeping language."[36]

Justice Thomas Dissents

In dissent, Justice Thomas wrote:

> The term in controversy here is "negligent transmission." The crux of my disagreement with the majority is its failure to assign the term "transmission" its plain meaning. That term is defined as the "[a]ct, operation, or process, of transmitting." Webster's New International Dictionary 2692 (2d ed. 1934, as republished 1945). "Transmit" is defined as, *inter alia*, "[t]o send or transfer

from one person or place to another; to forward by rail, post, wire, etc.,... [t]o cause... to pass or be conveyed." *Id.*, at 2692–2693. There is no cause to conclude that Congress was unaware of the ordinary definition of the terms "transmission" and "transmit" when it enacted the FTCA and the postal exception in 1946. Nor is there textual indication that Congress intended to deviate from the ordinary meaning of these terms. Accordingly, I would interpret the term "transmission" consistent with its ordinary meaning, and conclude that the postal exception exempts the Government from liability for *any* claim arising out of the negligent delivery of the mail to a Postal Service patron, including Dolan's slip-and-fall claim.[37]

A Brief Comment

In thinking about the approaches to statutory interpretation, the *Raila* and *Dolan* decisions are instructive. The Second Circuit's decision and the Supreme Court's decision sought to discern congressional meaning by understanding the context in which Congress legislated, focusing on common-sense construction of the words of the statute, keeping in mind a standard and well-applied concept embodied in the canon of *noscitur a sociis*—a word is given more precise content by the neighboring words with which it is associated. Indeed, Gluck and Bressman's empirical study of legislative drafting confirms that while drafters may not use the formal term *noscitur a sociis*, they are familiar with it and routinely apply it.[38] In undertaking our interpretive task, my panel sought to understand the real-world purpose of the statutes; we performed a reality test of sorts, noting the absurdity of other interpretations resulting from a purely textual approach, and the Supreme Court majority, with Justice Thomas disagreeing, supported that reality testing. In Judge

Richard Posner's words, a "judge should try to put himself in the shoes of the enacting legislators."[39] If that is not possible, "then the judge must decide what attribution of meaning...will yield the most reasonable result...bearing in mind...that it is [the legislators'] conception of reasonableness, to the extent known, rather than the judge's, that should guide decision."[40]

B. *UNITED STATES V. GAYLE*, 342 F.3D 89 (2D CIR. 2003), ENDORSED BY THE SUPREME COURT IN *SMALL V. UNITED STATES*, 544 U.S. 385 (2005)

Textualism's Limits: Whether "any court" in the phrase "convicted in any court" means courts in the United States only

In *United States v. Gayle*, our panel (Joseph McLaughlin, Pierre N. Leval, and I) faced a statutory question for which there was no obvious answer—whether "convicted in any court" pertains to a conviction only in a court in the United States, or to a conviction in any court in the world. Arguments could be marshaled on both sides. Looking only at the text or to a dictionary could not provide a compelling key to interpretation—indeed, it could result in an interpretation that Congress did not mean. Thus, in this close case of statutory construction, we went beyond the text to examine context, including legislative history. Ultimately, the Supreme Court resolved the matter.

The basic facts were these. Rohan Ingram, who was a defendant along with Kirk Gayle and Ann-Marie Richardson, was arrested in a Plattsburgh, New York, hotel upon suspicion that he had illegally entered the United States from Canada. Soon after his arrest, authorities found a large quantity of firearms stored in boxes in his hotel room. Ingram was later charged with conspiracy to export defense articles designated on the United States Munitions List; conspiracy to travel with intent to engage in the illegal acquisition of firearms; and being a felon in possession of a firearm, in violation of 18 U.S.C. §§ 922(g)(1), 924(a)(2). A jury found Ingram guilty on all three counts.

The offense underlying the felon-in-possession count was Ingram's 1996 conviction in Canada for violating § 85(1)(a) of the Canadian Criminal Code for use of a firearm in the commission of an indictable offense. Ingram's lawyers moved to dismiss the felon-in-possession count, arguing that, because his prior felony conviction did not occur in the United States, Ingram was not a felon within the meaning of the statute. The district judge concluded that § 922(g)(1)'s "in any court" language unambiguously includes foreign courts and thus held that Ingram's prior Canadian conviction was a proper predicate offense for § 922(g)(1).[41] The district court's decision was then appealed to the Court of Appeals.

The federal felon-in-possession statute was enacted as part of the Gun Control Act of 1968,[42] which states in relevant part:

> (g) It shall be unlawful for any person—
> (1) who has been *convicted in any court* of, a crime punishable by imprisonment for a term exceeding one year; ...
> to ship or transport in interstate or foreign commerce, or possess in or affecting commerce, any firearm or ammunition; or to receive any firearm or ammunition which has been shipped or transported in interstate or foreign commerce.[43]

If Ingram's Canadian conviction had been entered by a United States court, it would have qualified under § 922(g)(1) as a predicate offense—an earlier offense that can be used to enhance a sentence levied for a later conviction—because the statute prohibits possession of a weapon by a person previously convicted of a crime "punishable by imprisonment for a term exceeding one year." The determinative issue therefore was whether the phrase "convicted in any court" refers solely to convictions by courts in the United States or includes foreign convictions as well.

The Third, Fourth, and Sixth Circuits, along with two district courts, had concluded that "in any court" includes foreign courts.[44] Conversely, the Tenth Circuit, invoking what is known as the rule of lenity—that a court construing an ambiguous criminal statute should resolve the ambiguity in favor of the defendant—concluded that § 922(g)(1)'s "in any court" language is sufficiently ambiguous that foreign convictions cannot serve as predicate offenses for sentencing enhancements under 18 U.S.C. § 924(e).[45]

Our panel focused first on the plain text, recognizing that if the plain text is unambiguous, our work usually ends there. Most of the courts that determined that "in any court" includes foreign courts have stressed what they viewed as the unambiguously expansive nature of the phrase. Looking at the dictionary, the Seventh Circuit, for example, emphasized the broad, all-encompassing nature of the phrase "in any court":

> Looking to section 922(g)(1), we find nothing that defines or limits the term "court," only a requirement that a conviction have been "in any court" in the course of prohibiting possession of firearms by a felon. Certainly "any court" includes a military court, the adjective "any" expanding the term "court" to include "one or some indiscriminately of whatever kind"; "one that is selected without restriction or limitation of choice"; or "all." Webster's Third New International Dictionary, 1991.[46]

In deciding the case before our panel, we recognized that this interpretation had some force, commenting that there are good reasons
why Congress might have wanted to include at least certain types of
foreign convictions. "As this legislation," our opinion says, "represents a Congressional response to the danger posed by firearms in
the hands of convicted felons, Congress might reasonably have
wished to prohibit firearms possession at least by those convicted in
foreign countries of crimes of violence."[47]

On the other hand, we said that had Congress envisioned
extending the prohibition to persons having foreign convictions, it
would in all likelihood have been troubled by whether the prohibition should apply to those convicted by procedures and methods
that did not conform to our minimum standards of justice or of
crimes the United States would not consider to be felonies, or indeed, crimes at all. For instance, Congress might not have wanted to
penalize those convicted of crimes that are anathema to our First
Amendment freedoms, such as failure to observe the commands of
a mandatory religion or criticizing the government. Congress like-
wise might have been troubled by applying "in any court" to foreign
convictions under laws that punish conduct far more severely than
our domestic law does; in Singapore, for example, an individual can
be imprisoned for up to three years for acts of vandalism, making
the crime a felony when it would not be so classified in the United
States. The complete silence of the statute on such questions further
contributed to our sense that its meaning was not clear and that it
might be appropriate to look beyond its words alone for guidance
as to its meaning.

Hence, our examination of what constitutes a predicate offense
under § 922(g)(1) did not end with the words "in any court." Drawing
on precedent, we noted that the text's meaning could best be understood by looking to the statutory scheme as a whole and placing the

particular provision within the context of that statute. In § 921, the Gun Control Act's general statutory definition section, Congress excluded from the definition of the sort of crimes that constitute predicate offenses for a § 922(g)(1) conviction "any *Federal* or *State* offenses pertaining to antitrust violations, unfair trade practices, restraints of trade, or other similar offenses relating to the regulation of business practices," regardless of whether such a crime was "punishable by imprisonment for a term exceeding one year."[48] In finding § 922(g)(1) ambiguous, the Tenth Circuit relied heavily on this statutory definition, which it believed would cause a "peculiar result" if "in any court" included foreign courts. As the Tenth Circuit noted, if "in any court" were to include foreign courts, "we would be left with the anomalous situation that fewer domestic crimes would be covered than would be foreign crimes."[49] Like the Tenth Circuit, we did not understand the logic whereby a person convicted of an antitrust violation in a foreign country would not be allowed to possess a firearm, yet a person convicted of the same antitrust violation in the United States would be allowed to possess one. At the very least, we thought that § 921(a)(20) injected doubt as to whether Congress intended foreign convictions to serve as predicate offenses.[50]

Even without reference to the problem resulting from the inclusion of foreign business offenses as predicate offenses, we thought the phrase "in any court" was ambiguous. For instance, it is not unreasonable to understand statutory references to officers, officials, and acts of government as meaning those of the particular government that enacted the law. Just as a state statute authorizing "a police officer" to make an arrest probably means a police officer of that state and does not include police officers from foreign nations, so it is reasonable to read § 922(g)(1)'s reference to convictions as referring to convictions by courts in the United States. On the other hand, as noted above, there are legitimate reasons why, in the case of violent crimes for example, Congress might have wished to include foreign convictions as predicate offenses under § 922(g)(1).

To resolve this textual ambiguity, we determined that we could consult legislative history and other tools of statutory construction to discern Congress's meaning. Resort to authoritative legislative history may be justified, our panel wrote, where there is an open question as to the meaning of a word or phrase in a statute, or where a statute is silent on an issue of fundamental importance to its correct application. As a general matter, said our opinion, we may consider reliable legislative history where, as in this case, the statute is susceptible to divergent understandings and, equally important, where authoritative legislative history helps us discern what Congress actually meant.[51]

We looked first to the Senate Judiciary Committee Report on the Gun Control Act, as committee reports are among "the most authoritative and reliable materials of legislative history."[52] We determined that the Senate Report strongly suggested that Congress did not intend foreign convictions to serve as predicate offenses under the felon-in-possession statute. The Senate Report explained the meaning of the term "felony" as follows: "The definition of the term 'felony,' as added by the committee, is a new provision. It means a Federal crime punishable by a term of imprisonment exceeding 1 year and in the case of State law, an offense determined by the laws of the State to be a felony."[53] The Senate Report thus, in our view, unmistakably contemplated felonies, for purposes of the Gun Control Act, to include only convictions in courts in the United States.

Further evidence of Congress's intent to exclude foreign convictions came from the Conference Report, and we noted that next to the statute itself, the most pervasive evidence of congressional intent comes from a conference report "[b]ecause," we wrote, "a conference report represents the final statement of terms agreed to by both houses."[54] The Conference Report adopted the House version of the bill, which contained the statute's current language, "crime punishable by imprisonment for a term exceeding one year."[55] According to our panel, however, the Conference Report voiced no disagreement with the Senate Report's explicit limitation of felonies to include only convictions attained in domestic courts. Rather, the Conference Report merely chose the phrase "crime punishable by imprisonment for a term exceeding 1 year" over the word "felony."[56] Moreover, nowhere did the Conference Report make any mention of foreign convictions serving as predicate offenses.

In sum, two reliable portions of the Gun Control Act's legislative history—the Senate Report and the Conference Report—led us to conclude that Congress did not intend foreign convictions to serve as a predicate offense for § 922(g)(1). Accordingly, we interpreted § 922(g)(1)'s ambiguous "convicted in any court" language as including only convictions attained in domestic courts and not extending to Ingram's Canadian conviction.

In reaching our decision, we noted that Congress has the power to enact gun control legislation that criminalizes firearm possession by individuals with foreign felony convictions: "If Congress were to do so, however, it would need to speak more clearly than it has in § 922(g)(1). Today, we only choose not to write into a statute a meaning that seems contrary to what Congress intended."[57]

The Supreme Court Approaches the Statutory Question: Small v. United States, 544 U.S. 385 (2005)

In concluding that "convicted in any court" did not include foreign convictions, our Second Circuit panel agreed with the Tenth Circuit and disagreed with the Third, Fourth, and Sixth Circuits.[58] The Supreme Court granted certiorari to resolve the circuit split. The Court held that "convicted in any court" encompasses only domestic, not foreign, convictions. Justice Breyer delivered the opinion of the Court, in which Justices Stevens, O'Connor, Souter, and Ginsburg joined. Justice Thomas filed a dissenting opinion in which Justices Scalia and Kennedy joined. Chief Justice William H. Rehnquist took no part in the decision of the case.

In the case that the Court chose to resolve the split, Small was convicted in a Japanese court of trying to smuggle firearms and ammunition into that country. He served five years in prison and then returned to the United States, where he bought a gun. Federal authorities subsequently charged Small under 18 U.S.C. § 922(g)(1), and Small pleaded guilty while reserving the right to challenge his conviction on the ground that his earlier conviction, being foreign, fell outside § 922(g)(1)'s scope. The federal district court and the Third Circuit rejected this argument.

Justice Breyer began by squarely presenting the problem of determining whether "convicted in *any* court" includes a conviction entered in a foreign court. He wrote:

> The word "any" considered alone cannot answer this question. In ordinary life, a speaker who says, "I'll see any film," may or may not mean to include films shown in another city. In law, a legislature that uses the statutory phrase " 'any person' " may or may not mean to include " 'persons' " outside "the jurisdiction of the state." Thus, even though the word "any" demands a broad interpretation, we must look beyond that word itself.[59]

In considering the scope of "convicted in any court," the Court said that it is appropriate to assume that Congress had domestic concerns in mind, similar to the presumption that Congress ordinarily intends its statutes to have domestic, not extraterritorial, application.[60] In this context, the phrase "convicted in any court" describes one necessary portion of the "gun possession" activity that is prohibited as a matter of domestic law. Moreover, opined Justice Breyer, foreign convictions may include convictions for conduct that domestic laws would permit (for example, for engaging in economic conduct that our society might encourage), convictions from a legal system that is inconsistent with an American understanding of fairness, and convictions for conduct that domestic law punishes far less severely. Thus, the key statutory phrase "convicted in any court of, a crime punishable by imprisonment for a term exceeding one year" somewhat less reliably identifies dangerous individuals for purposes of U.S. law where foreign convictions, rather than domestic convictions, are at issue. In addition, the majority determined, it is difficult to read the statute as asking judges or prosecutors to refine its definitional distinctions where foreign convictions are at issue. The Court said that "[t]o somehow weed out inappropriate foreign convictions that meet the statutory definition is not consistent with the statute's language; it is not easy for those not versed in foreign laws to accomplish; and it would leave those previously convicted in a foreign court (say, of economic crimes) uncertain about their legal obligations."[61] These considerations, Justice Breyer stated, provided a convincing basis for applying here the ordinary assumption that domestically oriented statutes apply only domestically. Thus, the Court assumed a congressional intent that the phrase "convicted in any court" applies domestically, not extraterritorially, unless the statutory language, context, history, or purpose were to the contrary.

The Court also stated that there was no convincing indication to the contrary here because the statute's language suggests no intent to reach beyond domestic convictions. If read to include foreign convictions, the statute's language creates anomalies. As had our panel, the Supreme Court noted that in creating an exception allowing gun possession despite a conviction for an antitrust or business regulatory crime, § 921(a)(20)(A) speaks of "Federal or State" antitrust or regulatory offenses. In the Court's view, if the phrase "convicted in any court" generally refers only to domestic convictions, this language causes no problem. But if the phrase includes foreign convictions, the words "Federal or State" would prevent the exception from applying where a *foreign* antitrust or regulatory conviction is at issue. Such illustrative examples suggest, Justice Breyer wrote, that Congress did not consider whether the generic phrase "convicted in any court" applies to foreign convictions.[62]

Moreover, the Court determined that the statute's legislative history indicated no intent to reach beyond domestic convictions. Although the statutory purpose of keeping guns from those likely to become a threat to society offers some support for reading § 922(g)(1) to include foreign convictions, the likelihood that Congress, at best, paid no attention to the matter is reinforced by the empirical fact that, according to the government, between 1968 and the time of the Supreme Court's consideration of this case, there had been fewer than a dozen instances in which such a foreign conviction had served as a predicate for a felon-in-possession prosecution.

Justice Thomas Dissents, Joined by Justices Scalia and Kennedy

In dissent, Justice Thomas wrote:

> The broad phrase "any court" unambiguously includes all judicial bodies with jurisdiction to impose the requisite conviction—a conviction for a crime punishable by imprisonment for a term of more than a year. Indisputably, Small was convicted in a Japanese court of crimes punishable by a prison term exceeding one year. The clear terms of the statute prohibit him from possessing a gun in the United States.[63]

He stated that, in contrast to other parts of the firearms-control law that expressly mention only state or federal law, "any court" is not qualified by jurisdiction. He rejected the Court's reasoning:

> Faced with the inescapably broad text, the Court narrows the statute by assuming that the text applies only to domestic convictions; criticizing the accuracy of foreign convictions as a proxy for dangerousness; finding that the broad, natural reading of the statute "creates anomalies"; and suggesting that Congress did not consider whether foreign convictions counted. None of these arguments is persuasive.[64]

Justice Thomas argued that the majority had inappropriately invented a canon of statutory interpretation limiting the reach of domestically oriented statutes. He wrote that it "was eminently reasonable" for Congress to use as proxy for dangerousness convictions punishable by imprisonment for more than a year, foreign no less than domestic. He also stated that the "rarity of such prosecutions...only refutes the Court's simultaneous claim that a parade of horribles will result if foreign convictions count."[65]

Justice Thomas also disagreed that the legislative history is silent, and interpreted the elimination in conference of the limiting references to "Federal" and "State" to mean that "not *only* federal and state convictions were meant to be covered."[66] In a bow to Justice Scalia, who joined the dissent but would object to reliance on legislative history, Justice Thomas stated:

> Some, of course, do not believe that any statement or text that has not been approved by both Houses of Congress and the President (if he signed the bill) is an appropriate source of statutory interpretation. But for those who do, this committee change

ought to be strong confirmation of the fact that "any" means not "any Federal or State," but simply "any."[67]

A Brief Comment

The question here was difficult; reflexively relying on the text could not supply the answer, nor could a dictionary. As reasonable arguments could be made on both sides, I had prepared a draft coming out the other way to sharpen my thinking. Our panel's opinion implicitly acknowledged the difficulty of this case by explicitly observing that Congress may seek to enact gun control legislation that criminalizes firearm possession by individuals with foreign felony convictions, but that if Congress were to do so, it would have to be clearer than it was in § 922(g)(1). Interpreting Congress's work as best we could, we were mindful that it was not our charge to write into a statute a meaning that seemed contrary to what Congress intended.

C. *MURPHY V. ARLINGTON CENTRAL SCHOOL DISTRICT BOARD OF EDUCATION*, 402 F.3D 332 (2D CIR. 2004), REVERSED BY THE SUPREME COURT, 548 U.S. 291 (2006)

The Value of Legislative History: Whether "reasonable attorneys' fees as part of the costs" includes expert consultant fees

Murphy v. Arlington Central School District Board of Education presented a matter of first impression in our circuit. My panel (Jon O. Newman, Rosemary Pooler, and I) had to interpret a provision of the Individuals with Disabilities Education Act ("IDEA"). We sought to understand the statute's purpose, drawing upon legislative history, Supreme Court precedent, the Supreme Court's citations to legislative history, and congressional activity. When the Supreme Court reversed our decision, it took a totally different tack, relying on arguments that lawyers for the school district raised for the first time when the case reached the Supreme Court. In contrast to the Supreme Court majority, for my panel and for the dissenting Justices, led by Justice Breyer, legislative history and understanding the flow of congressional action were vital in the interpretive process.

At issue in *Murphy* was whether parents who prevailed in disputes with their school systems over the educational placements of their disabled children were entitled to reimbursement for costs associated with hiring expert witnesses and consultants who aided them in the litigation.

The school board conceded that the parents were the prevailing party and that they were entitled to attorneys' fees under a provision of the IDEA authorizing a court to award "reasonable attorneys' fees as part of the costs" to parents who prevail in their complaints against their school boards.[68] However, school officials argued in the district court that the fee-shifting provisions were applicable to recovery of attorneys' fees only. The district court ruled against the school district's position and determined that consultant fees could be considered costs within the meaning of the Act.

The case then wended its way to the Court of Appeals, where the parents, Pearl and Theodore Murphy, represented themselves pro se, as they had in the district court, and Public Citizen, a national public interest law firm, participated as a friend of the court (amicus curiae).

In deciding the case, we stated: "While we appreciate—and in practice honor, wherever possible—the virtues of relying solely on statutory text, at times text without context can lead to results that Congress did not intend."[69] In our view, although "costs" is a term of art that generally does not include expert fees in civil rights fee-shifting statutes, we believed that Supreme Court precedent, the legislative history of the IDEA upon which the Supreme Court relied in its 1991 decision in *West Virginia University Hospitals, Inc. v. Casey*,[70] and congressional action in the aftermath of the Supreme Court's ruling in that case required us to find that Congress intended to and did authorize the reimbursement of expert fees in IDEA actions.

By way of background, in a 1987 case, the Supreme Court, addressing fee-shifting for expert witnesses under Federal of Civil Procedure 54(d) in an antitrust case, held that "when a prevailing party seeks reimbursement for fees paid to its own expert witnesses, a federal court is bound by the limit of [28 U.S.C.] § 1821(b), absent contract or explicit statutory authority to the contrary."[71] Under § 1821(b), witnesses' fees are limited to $40 per day for each day's attendance. Four years later, in *Casey*, the Supreme Court employed the same analysis in construing the fee-shifting provisions of civil rights statutes. Specifically, the Court held that while a prevailing party could recover "a reasonable attorney's fee as part of the costs" in civil rights actions, a prevailing party could *not* recover "expert fees" under 42 U.S.C. § 1988, because there was no "explicit statutory authority" indicating that Congress intended for that sort of fee-shifting.[72]

Notably, in reaching this result, the Court expressly compared and contrasted § 1988 to the IDEA. The Court observed in dicta (language not part of the holding, that is, the legal principle derived from the decision) that a conference committee report on the IDEA stated that "[t]he conferees intend that the term 'attorneys' fees as part of the costs' include reasonable expenses and fees of expert witnesses and the reasonable costs of any test or evaluation which is found to be necessary for the preparation of the...case."[73] Justice

Scalia, author of the majority opinion in *Casey*, acknowledged that "[t]he statement is an apparent effort to *depart* from ordinary meaning and to define a term of art."[74]

Our panel believed that this dicta, with its reference to the IDEA conference committee report, favored a construction of the IDEA providing for the reimbursement of costs such as those the Murphys incurred for an expert evaluation. To us, the Supreme Court itself had strongly intimated that the IDEA is different from ordinary fee-shifting statutes because the legislative history of the IDEA unambiguously indicates that Congress intended to *allow* recovery of the costs of experts, rather than *prevent* it.

In *Casey*, we thought, the Supreme Court signaled to Congress that if it wished for expert witness fees to be awarded as costs under § 1988, it would have to amend the then-existing § 1988, but that no such action was necessary with regard to IDEA expert witness fees because the conference committee report indicated that such expert witness fees were authorized as part of costs under the law. We therefore found it instructive that shortly after the Court's decision in *Casey*, Congress amended § 1988 in order to make expert fees compensable in civil rights actions, but Congress took no similar action with respect to the IDEA.[75] We believed it reasonable to infer that Congress, on the basis of the Supreme Court's *Casey* decision, saw no need to amend the IDEA because the Court had recognized that, in enacting the IDEA, Congress had sufficiently indicated in the conference committee report that prevailing parties could recover expert fees under the Act. And we noted that it is not as if Congress merely failed to amend the IDEA, having done so at the time of our opinion a number of times since *Casey*, most recently in December 2004.[76]

To those who would question our resort to legislative history, we observed that it was Justice Scalia, a noted skeptic of the use of legislative history, who authored *Casey*'s dicta about the apparent effort by Congress to depart from the ordinary meaning of the term "costs" in the IDEA. We also recognized that, while some legislative history is less reliable than others, a conference committee report is generally among the most authoritative. We considered the conference committee report here, given the Supreme Court's acceptance of it, the general reliability of the conference committee report itself, and the settled legislative expectations in the wake of the *Casey* decision.

We were also of the view that our holding was consistent with the purposes of the IDEA, which are to "ensure that all children with disabilities have available to them a free appropriate public education that emphasizes special education and related services designed to meet their unique needs and prepare them for further education, employment, and independent living" and "to ensure that the rights of children with disabilities and parents of such children are protected."[77] Expert testimony is often critical in IDEA cases, which entail fact-intensive inquiries about the child's disability and the effectiveness of the measures that the school board has offered to secure a free appropriate public education. The IDEA's procedural safeguards ensure that children and parents can realize whatever benefits are due. Thus, for example, we noted that parties to IDEA proceedings have "the right to be accompanied and advised by counsel and by individuals with special knowledge or training with respect to the problems of children with disabilities,"[78] and "[i]n any action or proceeding brought under this section, the court, in its discretion, may award reasonable attorneys' fees as part of the costs[] to a prevailing party who is the parent of a child with a disability."[79] We thought it would be inconsistent with the IDEA's conferral of the right to be accompanied by an "individual[] with special knowledge" to find that the IDEA's fee-shifting provision barred compensation for such an individual's service. Moreover, a prevailing plaintiff in an IDEA case, in contrast to plaintiffs in cases brought under other civil rights statutes, can collect no money damages; rather, their relief rests solely in the appropriate education of their child. Absent a fee-shifting provision that allows for the recovery of appropriate expert fees, most parents of children with disabilities would have difficulty pursuing their cases. Prohibiting expert witness fees for prevailing parents would thus frustrate the purposes of the IDEA, resulting in fewer children receiving the education they deserve.[80]

The Supreme Court Decides: Arlington Central School District Board of Education v. Murphy, 548 U.S. 291 (2006)

We thus joined the Third Circuit in its view that the IDEA provided for expert witness fees for prevailing parents.[81] In contrast, the Seventh and Eighth Circuits read the IDEA to limit recovery to attorneys' fees, because other costs were not defined and the statute did not explicitly award fees for expert witnesses or consultants.[82] To resolve the circuit split, the Supreme Court heard the appeal in *Murphy*. Writing for the Supreme Court in its 6-to-3 decision (Chief Justice Roberts and Justices Scalia, Kennedy, Ginsburg, Thomas, and Alito in the majority; Justices Stevens, Souter, and Breyer in the minority), Justice Alito reversed and ruled in favor of the school board.

Before the Supreme Court, the school board argued for the first time in the litigation that the Spending Clause of the Constitution essentially dictated an outcome in its favor. The Court agreed, determining that because the IDEA was enacted under the Spending Clause, school boards were responsible only for those fees about which the Act provided clear notice. Because the text of the IDEA did not refer to fees for expert witnesses or consultants, the Court concluded that states and school districts lacked the requisite notice that they could be responsible for such costs. Moreover, the Court asserted that although the IDEA addresses how courts should calculate attorneys' fees to ensure their reasonableness, Congress provided no similar language for expert witnesses and consultants.

In its analysis, the Court rejected the parents' and our panel's view that the language in the conference committee report accompanying the bill—"The conferees intend that the term 'attorneys' fees as part of the costs' include reasonable expenses and fees of expert witnesses"—meant that Congress intended that fees for expert witnesses should be recoverable to the same extent as attorneys' fees. The Court concluded that this mention of fees for expert witnesses was insufficient to counter what it considered to be "the unambiguous text" of the IDEA, which led it to reject the Murphys' claim for reimbursement:

> Whatever weight this legislative history would merit in another context, it is not sufficient here. Putting the legislative history aside, we see virtually no support for respondents' position. Under these circumstances, where everything other than the legislative history overwhelmingly suggests that expert fees may not be recovered, the legislative history is simply not enough. In a Spending Clause case, the key is not what a majority of the Members of both Houses intend but what the States are clearly told regarding the conditions that go along with the acceptance of those funds.[83]

The Court also differed with our panel's interpretation of Justice Scalia's dicta in *Casey* about the apparent effort by Congress to depart from the ordinary meaning of the term "costs" in the IDEA. Justice Alito wrote:

> The footnote did not state that the Conference Committee Report set out the correct interpretation of § 1415(i)(3)(B),

much less that the Report was sufficient, despite the language of the statute, to provide the clear notice required under the Spending Clause. The thrust of the footnote was simply that the term "attorneys' fees," standing alone, is generally not understood as encompassing expert fees.[84]

Justice Ginsburg agreed with the Court's holding but parted company with its reasoning as to the Spending Clause. She wrote that the "clear notice" requirement was not applicable in this case. Rather, she argued that the case could be resolved by reading the IDEA's text, which lacked any reference to fees for expert witnesses and consultants.[85]

Justice Breyer Dissents, Joined by Justices Stevens and Souter

In dissent, Justice Breyer began:

> Unlike the Court, I believe that the word "costs" includes, and authorizes payment of, the costs of experts. The word "costs" does not define its own scope. Neither does the phrase "attorneys' fees as part of costs." But Members of Congress did make clear their intent by, among other things, approving a Conference Report that specified that "the term 'attorneys' fees as part of the costs' include[s] reasonable expenses and fees of expert witnesses and the reasonable costs of any test or evaluation which is found to be necessary for the preparation of the parent or guardian's case in the action or proceeding." No Senator or Representative voiced *any* opposition to this statement in the discussion preceding the vote on the Conference Report—the last vote on the bill before it was sent to the President. I can find no good reason for this Court to interpret the language of this

statute as meaning the precise opposite of what Congress told us it intended.[86]

Justice Breyer undertook an extensive analysis of the provision's legislative history, with particular reference to the Conference Report, to support his view that Congress intended that expert fees be included as part of costs. He noted that when Congress amended the IDEA to add the fee-shifting provision in question, it directed the GAO to undertake a study that included tabulation of statistics about the costs of experts, which, he said, made it clear that Congress intended "costs" to mean more than attorneys' fees. Finally, Justice Breyer said the IDEA's purpose is to enable parents to advocate for their children, adding:

> [O]ur ultimate judicial goal is to interpret language in light of the statute's purpose. Only by seeking that purpose can we avoid the substitution of judicial for legislative will. Only by reading language in its light can we maintain the democratic link between voters, legislators, statutes, and ultimate implementation, upon which the legitimacy of our constitutional system rests.... [W]e must retain all traditional interpretive tools—text, structure, history, and purpose. And, because faithful interpretation is art as well as science, we cannot, through rule or canon, rule out the use of any of these tools, automatically and in advance.[87]

In short, he said, "[b]y disregarding a clear statement in a legislative Report adopted without opposition in both Houses of Congress, the majority has reached a result no Member of Congress expected or overtly desired. It has adopted an interpretation that undercuts, rather than furthers, the statute's purpose, a 'free' and 'appropriate' public education for 'all' children with disabilities. And it has adopted an approach that, I fear, divorces law from life."[88]

In a short dissent, Justice Souter underscored that a congressionally mandated study led him to agree with Justice Breyer that it was appropriate to look to legislative history in finding that Congress intended to include expert fees as recoverable costs.[89]

A Brief Comment

In *Arlington Central School District*, the disagreement between the Supreme Court majority and minority was about the importance to be assigned to the Spending Clause and how best to understand congressional purpose. The minority's examination of legislative history, much like my panel's, reflects a view that authoritative legislative materials are not only useful, but also what legislators expect interpreters to consider in seeking to fully understand legislative meaning. Here, the legislative history seemed to be a decisive indicator of what Congress meant to do. And also relevant, my panel thought, but also to little effect, was how Congress responded in the wake of the Supreme Court's *Casey* decision. Moreover, *Arlington Central School District* illustrates that the Supreme Court can decide a case based on arguments raised even late in the process; the prevailing party in the lower courts devoted scant attention to the Spending Clause arguments, in fact, arguing in its brief to the Supreme Court that by not raising those arguments, the School Board was precluded from doing so before the Supreme Court.

D. CODA

These cases show how other judges and I seek to resolve often difficult questions of statutory interpretation. As I noted at the outset of this chapter, we are aided by a wide range of instruments, such as the

text, statutory structure, history, word usage in other relevant statutes, common law usages, agency interpretations, dictionary definitions, technical and scientific usages, lay usages, canons, common
practices, and purpose. A reader who will be satisfied only by a
grand theory of statutory interpretation is no doubt disappointed.
I am inclined to the view that any grand theory will fail to capture
the nuances of the legislative process which undergirds our inquiry.
As Professor Kent Greenawalt has written, "multiple considerations
are relevant for statutory interpretation and...no neat categoriza-
tion of these can consistently produce simple answers when the
force of statutory language is not evident."[90] I hope that the cases
provided you a sense of the very concrete challenges before me,
challenges that do not lend themselves to a one-size-fits-all solution.
Statutes differ, contexts differ, and how tools are used may vary from
case to case. But the essential framework that guides me remains the
same: at all times, I seek to interpret the statute in ways that realize
Congress's meanings and purposes to the best I can discern them. It
is for me a practical inquiry, grounded in a process that is respectful
of the legislature and its workways. And, in that examination, sticking only to the text may stand in the way of correctly construing
legislative meaning. It is for you to judge whether I got it right.

Chapter 6

Promoting Understanding

My experience as a judge only reinforces my view that at some basic level, each institution—that is, the courts and the legislature—could benefit from a deeper appreciation of how the other operates. Congress, which enacts the laws, should find it useful to learn more about how the judiciary interprets its laws; and the judiciary, for its part, could learn more about the legislative process to better equip judges to interpret those laws. The lineage of jurists with legislative experience is a distinguished one, including England's Lord Mansfield in the eighteenth century.[1] Today—in contrast to a generation ago—only two federal judges have served as members of Congress.[2] And in Congress, there is only one former federal judge and one state supreme court justice, though some federal legislators clerked for judges.[3]

To aid the judiciary in understanding Congress, some entity such as the Congressional Research Service of the Library of Congress, perhaps in conjunction with the legislative counsels' offices in both legislative chambers, could sponsor periodic seminars for judges and law clerks about the legislative process, perhaps developing a manual and videos about the lawmaking process. A start on this task is a pamphlet for judges on legislative drafting conventions by M. Douglass Bellis, longtime member of the House legislative counsel's office.[4] Similarly, to help Congress understand how the courts work, the Federal Judicial Center and the Administrative

Office of the U.S. Courts could develop programs for legislators and their staffs about how the judiciary functions. Optimally, such activities could be incorporated into orientation programs for new judges, legislators, and staffs.

While mutual appreciation and deeper knowledge are always desirable, it would, of course, be fanciful to think that Congress would—or even could—do away with ambiguity in its laws. As I noted earlier, ambiguity may be a deliberate strategy to secure the necessary votes, or a product of the policy and political challenges surrounding the problem at hand.[5] Nevertheless, there may be ways for Congress to help clarify legislative meaning, through both the drafting and the statutory revision processes, as well as the development of more reliable legislative histories that could aid judges as they undertake their work. And in so doing, Congress can make it more likely that the "[d]ignity of [l]egislation,"[6] in Jeremy Waldron's felicitous phrase, will be preserved and respected.

A. DRAFTING AND STATUTORY REVISION

Ideally, legislators and their staffs should make greater use of the skilled legislative drafters in their offices of legislative counsel. If all legislative drafting were funneled through those offices, which apply accepted linguistic conventions and standards, then courts would have an easier time interpreting statutes. But that is not the reality of the legislative process. For those who do not avail themselves of the legislative drafting services, a checklist of common issues might be prepared—for example, dealing with such matters as attorneys' fees, private rights of action, preemption, statutes of limitations, effective dates, and exhaustion of administrative remedies. There have already been several proposals for such a checklist.[7] When not addressed in the law, such issues are resolved in court. While such a checklist would not prevent strategic, deliberate omissions, it could be useful in avoiding drafting oversights, clarifying legislative intent, and reducing burdens on the courts.

Similarly, the offices of legislative counsel could prepare a drafting guidebook for members and staffs. Law schools or some other neutral body could organize seminars with legislative counsels and judges to discuss problems of drafting and interpretation. Law school courses and continuing legal education programs on drafting would also be helpful, not only for those who work in Congress, but also for those in interest groups and organizations urging legislators and staffs to introduce bills for which they have crafted language.

Finally, to provide more precision, Congress might resort more to default rules, which would become effective when the legislative branch has not dealt with the particular issue in question in a specific substantive statute. For example, a statute may not explicitly provide for the time period in which a lawsuit must commence after the alleged violation of the law occurs. The failure to do so could lead to litigation, calling on courts to determine that time period. But a default rule enacted by Congress, as to civil statutes, solves the problem in circumstances where the specific law does not address the issue: "Except as otherwise provided by law, a civil action arising under an Act of Congress enacted after the date of the enactment of this section may not be commenced later than 4 years after the cause of action accrues."[8] Hence, the default position is triggered if a particular statute has not addressed the time limitations on the commencement of civil actions arising under it.

The flip side of drafting before bills are enacted is the statutory revision process. Interbranch understanding of statutes can also be enhanced through the process of statutory revision. Supreme Court justices will from time to time identify an opinion meriting further congressional attention, as Justice Ginsburg did, to prominent effect, in the Lilly Ledbetter case.[9] Congress is generally aware of Supreme Court decisions, as evidenced by legislative reversals of decisions of our highest tribunal.[10] But the first branch tends to give little attention to the large number of statutory opinions of the lower courts. This lack of attention, while understandable given Congress's workload, is curious in view of the role that those courts play in construing statutes. Since the Supreme Court hears about eighty cases a year, the decisions made in the federal appellate courts are especially consequential.

"Most of the work currently done by federal courts, including the Supreme Court," commented Justice Ginsburg, "involves not grand constitutional principle, but the interpretation and application of laws passed by Congress, laws that are sometimes ambiguous or obscure."[11] She further observed:

> When Congress is not clear, courts often invite, and are glad to receive, legislative correction. The law Congress declares, as the Chief Justice recently stated, is by and large the law federal courts apply. When Congress has been Delphic or dense, or simply imprecise, legislative clarification can ward off further confusion.[12]

Nearly five decades ago, Judge Henry J. Friendly of the Second Circuit, writing about the importance of statutory law, lamented "the problems posed by defective draftsmanship," especially in uncontroversial legislation.[13] He wrote about "the occasional statute in which the legislature has succeeded in literally saying something it probably did not mean,"[14] observed that "even the best draftsman is likely to have experienced the occasional shock of finding that what he wrote was not at all what he meant,"[15] and commented on the legislative time pressures that result in "neglect of the undramatic type of legislative activity."[16] Three decades later, another circuit judge, James L. Buckley of the D.C. Circuit and also a former senator, remembered that in Congress, "[w]ith time often the enemy, mistakes—problems of grammar, syntax, and punctuation—are made in the drafting of statutes and affect the meaning of legislation."[17]

Over the years, several proposals have been made to facilitate statutory revision.[18] Then–Circuit Judge Ginsburg and her coauthor Peter W. Huber recommended that a "second look at laws" committee be created, and that the Office of Law Revision Counsel, which has had a ministerial role of correcting citations, assist in "statutory housekeeping."[19] Judge Frank M. Coffin urged that a unit within the judiciary collate and sift judicial opinions with suggestions for the legislative branch and send them to Congress.[20] Then–Chief Judge James L. Oakes of the U.S. Court of Appeals for the Second Circuit, my court, seconded the proposal.[21] Judge Wilfred Feinberg of the same court called for the Judicial Conference to "designate a handful of law professors working on a part-time basis as a committee to call attention to... conflicts [among the circuits]."[22] Justice Stevens suggested that Congress create a legislative mechanism to resolve intercircuit conflicts.[23]

These thoughts have a distinguished lineage. In 1921, Benjamin N. Cardozo, then an associate judge on the New York Court of Appeals, drawing upon Roscoe Pound and Jeremy Bentham, recommended the creation of ministries of justice to facilitate law revision.[24] In the early 1960s, Judge Friendly stated that "[i]t would seem elementary that an agency whose task is to [help] formulate legislation... should be attached to the legislature."[25]

One approach that promotes improved drafting and that may also lead to statutory revision is a practical effort, in which I participated, designed over twenty years ago by the Governance Institute.[26] Through this project of "statutory housekeeping"[27]—in Justice Ginsburg's apt phrase—courts of appeals send opinions that identify possible technical problems in statutes to Congress for its information and for whatever action it wishes to take.[28] The effort informs the drafters as well as legislators and staff more generally of the technical problems that judges identify in opinions applying statutes.

The project began in 1988 when some judges of the U.S. Court of Appeals for the D.C. Circuit invited Judge Coffin, then chair of the Judicial Conference's Judicial Branch Committee, and me[29] to analyze what happened in Congress after the courts issued statutory decisions that referred to problems in grammar, apparent "glitches," ambiguous terminology, and omissions of key details, such as effective dates.[30] With the aid of the D.C. Circuit judges, after identifying a small body of relevant opinions, we assessed legislative awareness of these opinions. We discovered that committee staff did not know about judicial opinions concerning technical aspects of the statutes under the committee's jurisdiction, although they were cognizant of decisions on broad, policy-oriented issues of statutory interpretation or decisions that a losing party with influence had asked Congress to reverse.[31]

Working with legislators and their staffs, we—with the counsel of Governance Institute Distinguished Fellow and former House member Robert W. Kastenmeier—conceived of a pilot project, whereby the D.C. Circuit Court of Appeals would transmit its relevant statutory opinions to the House of Representatives.[32] In 1993, Chief Justice Rehnquist backed the pilot project,[33] and two years later the Judicial Conference recommended that all courts of appeals participate.[34]

In the early 2000s, more than half the courts of appeals had transmitted opinions to Congress. Participation declined, however, because the project had not been fully institutionalized within the judiciary. In May 2006, the legislative counsels of Congress asked the Governance Institute, led by Russell R. Wheeler, to revitalize the project.[35] The result was a July 2007 memorandum from the Director of the Administrative Office of the U.S. Courts, James Duff, and from the leadership of the U.S. Judicial Conference Committee on the Judicial Branch, to all circuit judges, along with letters from the bipartisan leadership of both Judiciary Committees, asking all courts of appeals to participate.[36] Opinions that are appropriate for transmission include those where the court has identified possible grammatical problems that affect meaning and where the statute requires courts to fill in a gap (for example, whether Congress intended the statute to be retroactive). They also include statutes that may present ambiguities in language or ambiguities arising from having to interpret related statutes, or statutes with a perceived problem, about which a judicial opinion suggests the possibility of legislative action.

The questions raised in the opinions[37] have been far-ranging. For instance, one opinion confronted the question of whether the Immigration and Nationality Act's requirement that an individual "lawfully resided continuously" for seven years, necessary for a waiver of inadmissibility, begins when an alien applies for adjustment of status or when that status is actually granted.[38] Another case examined whether, pursuant to Chapter 13 of the U.S. Bankruptcy Code, debtors who own rather than lease a vehicle may deduct ownership costs from bankruptcy repayment plans.[39] In still another example, the Seventh Circuit considered whether the Sex Offender Registration and Notification Act's registration requirement applies to offenders whose travel occurred before the Act's passage[40] (a gap that the Supreme Court resolved in *Carr v. United States*[41]) and whether conviction for failure to register requires evidence that the defendant "knowingly" violated the registration provision.[42]

Grappling with a provision in the Class Action Fairness Act of 2005,[43] appellate courts split as to the meaning of "not less than 7 days after the entry of the order" where a court of appeals "may accept an appeal from an order of a district court granting or denying a motion to remand a class action [that is, to send that case back to the state court]...if application is made to the court of appeals not less than 7 days after entry of the order."[44] The Third Circuit read the statute as meaning "not more than,"[45] while the Seventh Circuit read the statute literally as meaning "not less than seven days."[46] Ultimately, Congress amended the section to read "not more than 10 days" after entry of the order.[47]

Under protocols worked out with legislative personnel, clerks of the courts of appeals send opinions identified by the clerk, staff attorney, or the three-judge panel to the House Speaker and Senate President Pro Tempore and to the chairs and ranking members of the two Judiciary Committees. The letter accompanying each opinion, which is in the nature of an executive communication, does not comment on the opinion; it says only: "Enclosed please find an opinion of the United States Court of Appeals for the [X] Circuit, which may be of interest to the Congress."[48] At the same time, the clerk sends electronic copies of the letters and opinions to the respective House and Senate legislative counsels, to Governance Institute President Russell R. Wheeler, and to Carol Messito, an attorney in the Office of the General Counsel in the Administrative Office of the U.S. Courts.[49] The legislative counsels use the opinions as teaching tools about how the courts of appeals deal with drafting problems.[50] The counsels' offices also transmit the opinions to the House and Senate committees with jurisdiction over the legislation in question for any action those committees may wish to take.[51]

Legislative support has been vital to this project throughout its history. Both legislative counsels participated enthusiastically in the pilot project.[52] Legislators themselves have been consistently positive.[53] More recently, in September 2010, in remarks to the Judicial Conference, Senator Jeff Sessions, then ranking member of the Senate Judiciary Committee, urged the participation of all circuits as a good government project.[54]

The strongest indicator of the project's value is the legislative testimonials calling for all courts of appeals to participate. Legislators and their staffs, including the offices of legislative counsel, have much to do. That they would call for all circuits to participate suggests that the transmitted opinions benefit the drafting process.

A second measure of the project's worth derives from the ways that the legislative counsels use the transmissions. Having examined how courts apply statutory language in specific contexts, the legislative counsels can be more sensitive to drafting issues that may result in litigation. Frank L. Burk, Jr., head of the Senate Office of Legislative Counsel in the 1990s, reported that the project "helped stimulate a comprehensive two-year review of the basic rules of legislative drafting"[55] by his office. He further stated that the office "developed a drafting manual that compiles the drafting rules and conventions identified during the review," and that the office used transmitted opinions as teaching devices for "beginning staff attorneys."[56] James Fransen, Burk's successor, has been similarly supportive.[57] House Legislative Counsel M. Pope Barrow concurred, observing that "[t]he opinions of judges would be especially useful if they can identify persistent patterns in drafting errors."[58] Deputy Legislative Counsel M. Douglass Bellis, who has overseen the project in the House for many years, has said: "The greater the communication between the judicial and legislative branches of government, the more the courts and Congress will grow to understand each other and the more the public can examine what its agents are doing on its behalf."[59] Both Bellis and Fransen circulate transmitted opinions to their respective staffs because of the opinions' instructive value.[60]

At first glance, one might think that the most important metric of the project's effectiveness would be the number of statutes passed to remedy problems identified in the opinions. From the outset, however, the project's creators cautioned that its principal purpose was not to produce legislative change, but rather to inform busy legislators and their staffs of possible technical problems in statutes. And, as Bellis noted, Congress may do nothing because it may determine that the relevant court "is making good decisions in hard cases,"[61] thereby creating no reason for Congress to intervene. The goal of the project "is not to find 'mistakes' that Congress made and should correct... [but] to open communication so that Congress can learn how the courts are reacting to and interpreting statutes."[62] He observed that the feedback is invaluable: "[I]t calls our attention to drafting situations that are capable of repetition," suggesting that the referrals may "have a greater ultimate influence on the language of statutes than when (and to the extent) they lead to an amendment of the particular law."[63]

In sum, the mechanism for transmitting opinions has the following virtues: (1) it is a neutral mechanism of communication, merely a transmission belt; (2) it does not require the creation of a body or committee; (3) Congress has encouraged it; and (4) it promotes good government. In the words of the chairs and ranking members of the House and Senate Judiciary Committees: "These modest efforts have supplied pertinent and timely information to Congress that it might not otherwise receive," including information about "possible technical problems in statutes that may be susceptible to technical amendment; and, in any case, how statutes might be drafted to reflect legislative intent most accurately."[64] Although it is inherent in the system that there will be occasional tensions between courts and Congress, this effort promotes interbranch comity and dialogue in a way that reduces conflict. Indeed, it may well be worth considering whether it might be useful to develop a parallel transmission process between the executive branch and Congress, whereby agency general counsels sifting through judicial opinions would identify issues of relevance to Congress, perhaps with suggestions for Congress to consider. The Administrative Conference of the United States,[65] of which I am a senior fellow, is exploring how it might play a useful role in examining the feasibility of this idea and its implementation.

B. MAKING LEGISLATIVE HISTORY MORE RELIABLE

In an era when Congress passes large omnibus bills that encompass a large number of diverse, often unrelated subjects, making legislative history more reliable is all the more important. To better signal a statute's meaning, legislative leadership could more clearly identify legislative history that courts should take into account. For instance, where feasible, the floor managers of a bill could indicate what constitutes the definitive legislative history, including floor statements and colloquies. Such signaling would simplify a court's task in reviewing the Congressional Record. Steven Charnovitz has suggested that the enrolled bill—the final copy of a bill or joint resolution which has passed both chambers in identical form, signed by the appropriate House and Senate officers and submitted to the President for signature—could also be a vehicle for conveying legislative history. In other words, accompanying the enrolled bill would be an official listing of legislative history, although, of course, the President would not be asked to sign the legislative history. Another idea relates to the use of THOMAS, online resource of the Library of Congress, launched by the leadership of the 104th Congress, to make federal legislative information freely available to the public. Under the direction of Congress, THOMAS could add a section, "Legislative History" that would consist, for example, of specific links to committee reports, relevant colloquies and floor statements, making it easier for courts to sift through such history.[66]

Moreover, as Stephen F. Ross proposed several years ago, having committee members sign committee reports, with signature sheets attached to the document, could effectively meet the charge that those reports are not endorsed by a majority of the committee. This could address the concern that committee members are not aware of the reports, or just do not read them.[67] At present, generally only those offering additional views sign the reports. Identifying authoritative legislative history, moreover, will make it easier for courts to assess amicus briefs of legislators that are filed to persuade the courts about what Congress meant in passing the statute. For legislators to try to achieve through such briefs what they could not in Congress itself is something Representative Kastenmeier deemed "a questionable procedure."[68] The more authoritative the legislative history is, the more likely it is that courts can review amicus briefs and interpret statutes in ways that do not result in what Senator Hatch called " 'slippage' from agreements reached in Congress."[69]

Congress and courts are together engaged in an ongoing venture. The better understood the legislature makes its laws through text and accompanying materials, the more likely that the judiciary will interpret those laws in ways consonant with congressional meaning.

Chapter 7

Conclusion

There you have it: the views of a judge, judging statutes. In the end, my points are simply these. In our constitutional system in which Congress, the people's branch, is charged with enacting laws, how Congress makes its purposes known—through text and reliable accompanying materials—should be respected, lest the integrity of legislation be undermined. The experience of the executive branch in interpreting statutes can be helpful to courts. And practical ways should be pursued to further the objective of promoting statutory understanding. With greater sensitivity to the workings of the branches in the lawmaking process, we will be closer to realizing Publius's (most likely Madison's) vision in *The Federalist* No. 62: "A good government implies two things: first, fidelity to the object of government, which is the happiness of the people[;] secondly, a knowledge of the means by which the object can be best attained."[1]

Statutes, after all, are expressions by the people's representatives of this nation's aspirations, its challenges, and approaches to those challenges. That has been so throughout our country's experience, across a whole range of issues, mundane and dramatic, bearing on the very fabric of our values. That has been true as Congress enacted laws, for example, addressing civil rights, the environment, health care, voting rights, the economy, national security, and gender discrimination. When judges interpret the words of statutes, they are not simply performing a task. They are maintaining an unspoken covenant with the citizenry on whose trust the authority and vitality of an independent judiciary depend, to render decisions that strive to be faithful to the work of the people's representatives memorialized in statutory language. To have a part in that system of constitutional governance is a great privilege, indeed.

APPENDIX A

Selected Commentary Over the Last Three Decades by Federal Judges on Statutory Construction

A. CONGRESSIONAL DOCUMENTS

Statutory Interpretation and the Uses of Legislative History: Hearing Before the Subcomm. on Courts, Intellectual Prop. & the Admin. of Justice of the H. Comm. on the Judiciary, 101st Cong. 24 (1990) (statement of James L. Buckley, J., U.S. Court of Appeals for the District of Columbia Circuit).

B. BOOKS AND ARTICLES IN COLLECTED WORKS

Stephen Breyer, Active Liberty: Interpreting Our Democratic Constitution 85–101 (New York: Knopf, 2005).

Stephen Breyer, Making Our Democracy Work: A Judge's View 88–105 (New York: Alfred A. Knopf, 2010).

Guido Calabresi, A Common Law for the Age of Statutes (Cambridge, MA: Harvard University Press, 1982).

Richard A. Posner, How Judges Think 191–203 (Cambridge, MA: Harvard University Press, 2008).

Richard A. Posner, Reflections on Judging (Cambridge, MA: Harvard University Press, 2013).

Antonin Scalia, *Common-Law Courts in a Civil-Law System*, in A Matter of Interpretation: Federal Courts and the Law 3, ed. Amy Gutmann (Princeton, NJ: Princeton University Press, 1997).

Antonin Scalia & Bryan A. Garner, Reading Law: The Interpretation of Legal Texts (St. Paul, MN: Thomson/West, 2012).

C. ARTICLES

Stephen Breyer, *On the Uses of Legislative History in Interpreting Statutes*, 65 S. Cal. L. Rev. 845 (1992).

Frank H. Easterbrook, *Judicial Discretion in Statutory Interpretation*, 57 Okla. L. Rev. 1 (2004).

Frank H. Easterbrook, *Statutes' Domains*, 50 U. Chi. L. Rev. 533 (1983).

Frank H. Easterbrook, *Text, History, and Structure in Statutory Interpretation*, 17 Harv. J.L. & Pub. Pol'y 61 (1994).

Ruth Bader Ginsburg, *Communicating and Commenting on the Court's Work*, 83 Geo. L.J. 2119 (1995).

Alex Kozinksi, *Should Reading Legislative History Be an Impeachable Offense?*, 31 Suffolk U. L. Rev. 807 (1998).

Pierre N. Leval, *Trademark: Champion of Free Speech*, 27 Colum. J.L. & Arts 187 (2004).

Diarmuid F. O'Scannlain, *Lawmaking and Interpretation: The Role of a Federal Judge in Our Constitutional Framework*, 91 Marq. L. Rev. 895 (2008).

Richard A. Posner, *Legal Formalism, Legal Realism, and the Interpretation of Statutes and the Constitution*, 37 Case W. Res. L. Rev. 179 (1986).

A. Raymond Randolph, *Dictionaries, Plain Meaning, and Context in Statutory Interpretation*, 17 Harv. J. L. & Pub. Pol'y 71 (1994).

Kenneth W. Starr & Abner J. Mikva, *Observations About the Use of Legislative History*, 1987 Duke L.J. 371.

John Paul Stevens, *Some Thoughts on Judicial Restraint*, 66 Judicature 177 (1982).

John M. Walker, Jr., *Judicial Tendencies in Statutory Construction: Differing Views of the Role of the Judge*, 58 N.Y.U. Ann. Surv. Am. L. 203 (2001).

Stephen F. Williams, *Restoring Context, Distorting Text: Legislative History and the Problem of Age*, 66 Geo. Wash. L. Rev. 1366 (1998).

Selected Commentary Since 1997 Addressing Statutory Interpretation

Since 1997, when I last surveyed the field in research for *Courts and Congress*, there have been hundreds of articles and many books addressing in some fashion statutory interpretation. Given the proposition that a subject matter's importance can in part be measured by the amount of attention paid to it, I list many of the articles and books here to establish that statutory interpretation is surely a matter of importance.

A. BOOKS

Michael A. Bailey & Forrest Maltzman, The Constrained Court: Law, Politics, and the Decisions Justices Make (Princeton, NJ: Princeton University Press, 2011).

William C. Burton, Burton's Legal Thesaurus, 5th ed. (New York: McGraw-Hill Professional, 2013).

Frank B. Cross, The Theory and Practice of Statutory Interpretation (Stanford, CA: Stanford University Press, 2009).

Einer Elhauge, Statutory Default Rules: How to Interpret Unclear Legislation (Cambridge, MA: Harvard University Press, 2008).

William N. Eskridge, Jr., Philip P. Frickey & Elizabeth Garrett, eds., Statutory Interpretation Stories (New York: Foundation Press, 2011).

William N. Eskridge, Jr. & John Ferejohn, A Republic of Statutes: The New American Constitution (New Haven, CT: Yale University Press 2010).

William N. Eskridge, Jr., Philip P. Frickey & Elizabeth Garrett, Cases and Materials on Legislation: Statutes and the Creation of Public Policy (West Group, 2007).

William N. Eskridge, Jr., Philip P. Frickey & Elizabeth Garrett, Legislation and Statutory Interpretation, 2d ed. (New York: Foundation Press, 2006).

Kent Greenawalt, Legislation: Statutory Interpretation: 20 Questions (New York: Foundation Press, 1999).

Kent Greenawalt, Statutory and Common Law Interpretation (New York: Oxford University Press, 2013).

John F. Manning & Matthew C. Stephenson, Legislation and Regulation, 2d ed. (New York: Foundation Press, 2013).

Abner J. Mikva & Eric Lane, Legislative Process, 3d ed. (New York: Wolters Kluwer Law & Business, 2009).

Jeffrey A. Segal, Harold J. Spaeth, & Sara C. Benesh, The Supreme Court in the American Legal System (New York: Cambridge University Press, 2005).

Lawrence Sloan, The Language of Statutes: Laws and Their Interpretation (Chicago: University of Chicago Press, 2010).

Peter L. Strauss, Legislation: Understanding and Using Statutes (New York: Foundation Press, 2006).

Adrian Vermeule, Judging Under Uncertainty: An Institutional Theory of Legal Interpretation (Cambridge, MA: Harvard University Press, 2006).

Jeremy Waldron, The Dignity of Legislation (New York: Cambridge University Press, 1999).

Jeremy Waldron, Law and Disagreement (New York: Oxford University Press, 1999).

B. ARTICLES

Bernard W. Bell, *Legislative History Without Legislative Intent: The Public Justification Approach to Statutory Interpretation*, 60 Ohio St. L.J. 1 (1999).

Andrew D. Bradt, *Resolving Intrastate Conflict of Laws: The Example of the Federal Arbritation Act*, 92 Wash. U. L. Rev. (forthcoming 2014).

Glenn Bridgman, *One of These Things Is Not Like the Others: Legislative History in the U.S. Courts of Appeal* (Yale Law Sch. Student Prize Papers, No. 88, 2012), *available at* http://digitalcommons.law.yale.edu/ylsspps_papers/88

James J. Brudney, *Below the Surface: Comparing Legislative History Usage by the House of Lords and the Supreme Court*, 85 Wash. U. L. Rev. 1 (2007).

James J. Brudney, *Canon Shortfalls and the Virtues of Political Branch Interpretive Assets*, 98 Calif. L. Rev. 1199 (2010).

James J. Brudney, *Confirmatory Legislative History*, 76 Brook. L. Rev. 901 (2011).

James J. Brudney, *Intentionalism's Revival*, 44 San Diego L. Rev. 1001 (2007).

James J. Brudney, *The Supreme Court as Interstitial Actor: Justice Ginsburg's Eclectic Approach to Statutory Interpretation*, 70 Ohio St. L.J. 889 (2009).

James J. Brudney & Lawrence Baum, *Oasis or Mirage: The Supreme Court's Thirst for Dictionaries in the Rehnquist and Roberts Eras*, 55 Wm. & Mary L. Rev. 483 (2013).

James J. Brudney & Corey Ditslear, *The Decline and Fall of Legislative History? Patterns of Supreme Court Reliance in the Burger and Rehnquist Eras*, 89 Judicature 220 (2006).

James J. Brudney & Corey Ditslear, *Liberal Justices' Reliance on Legislative History: Principle, Strategy, and the Scalia Effect*, 29 Berkeley J. Emp. & Lab. L. 117 (2008).

James J. Brudney & Corey Ditslear, *The Warp and Woof of Statutory Interpretation: Comparing Supreme Court Approaches in Tax Law and Workplace Law*, 58 Duke L.J. 1231 (2009).

William W. Buzbee, *The One-Congress Fiction in Statutory Interpretation*, 149 U. Pa. L. Rev. 171 (2000).

Carol Chomsky, *The Story of Holy Trinity Church v. United States (1892): Spirit and History in Statutory Interpretation* in Statutory Interpretation Stories (William N. Eskridge, Jr., Philip P. Frickey & Elizabeth Garrett eds.) 2–35 (New York: Foundation Press, 2011).

Matthew R. Christiansen & William N. Eskridge, Jr., *Congressional Overrides of Supreme Court Statutory Interpretation Decisions, 1967–2011*, 92 Tex. L. Rev. 1317 (2014).

Maura D. Corrigan & J. Michael Thomas, *"Dice Loading" Rules of Statutory Interpretation*, 59 N.Y.U. Ann. Surv. Am. L. 231 (2003).

Frank B. Cross, *The Significance of Statutory Interpretive Methodologies*, 82 Notre Dame L. Rev. 1971 (2007).

Einer Elhauge, *Preference-Eliciting Statutory Default Rules*, 102 Colum. L. Rev. 2162 (2002).

Anthony L. Engel, Note, *Questionable Uses of Canons of Statutory Interpretation: Why the Supreme Court Erred When It Decided "Any" Only Means "Some,"* 96 J. Crim. L. & Criminology 877 (2006).

William N. Eskridge, Jr., *All About Words: Early Understandings of the "Judicial Power" in Statutory Interpretation, 1776–1806*, 101 Colum. L. Rev. 990 (2001).

William N. Eskridge, Jr., *The New Textualism and Normative Canons*, 113 Colum. L. Rev. 531 (2013).

William N. Eskridge, Jr., *Should the Supreme Court Read* The Federalist *but Not Statutory Legislative History?*, 66 Geo. Wash. L. Rev. 1301 (1998).

William N. Eskridge, Jr. & Lauren E. Baer, *The Continuum of Deference: Supreme Court Treatment of Agency Statutory Interpretations from Chevron to Hamdan*, 96 Geo. L.J. 1083 (2008).

Daniel A. Farber, *Do Theories of Statutory Interpretation Matter? A Case Study*, 94 Nw. U. L. Rev. 1409 (2000).

Philip P. Frickey, *Interpretive-Regime Change*, 38 Loy. L.A. L. Rev. 1971 (2005).

Amanda Frost, *Certifying Questions to Congress*, 101 Nw. U. L. Rev. 1 (2007).

Elizabeth Garrett, *The Story of TVA v. Hill (1973): Congress Has the Last Word*, in Statutory Interpretation Stories (William N. Eskridge, Jr., Philip P. Frickey & Elizabeth Garrett eds.) 58–91 (New York: Foundation Press, 2011).

Abbe R. Gluck, *The States as Laboratories of Statutory Interpretation: Methodological Consensus and the New Modified Textualism*, 119 Yale L.J. 1750 (2010).

Abbe R. Gluck & Lisa Schultz Bressman, *Statutory Interpretation From the Inside— An Empirical Study of Congressional Drafting, Delegation and the Canons: Part I*, 65 Stan. L. Rev. 901 (2013).

Abbe R. Gluck & Lisa Schultz Bressman, *Statutory Interpretation From the Inside— An Empirical Study of Congressional Drafting, Delegation and the Canons: Part II*, 66 Stan. L. Rev. 725 (2014).

Senator Charles Grassley & Jennifer Shaw Schmidt, Policy Essay, *Practicing What We Preach: A Legislative History of Congressional Accountability*, 35 Harv. J. on Legis. 33 (1998).

Abner S. Greene, *The Missing Step of Textualism*, 74 Fordham L. Rev. 1913 (2006).

Robert J. Gregory, *Overcoming Text in an Age of Textualism: A Practitioner's Guide to Arguing Cases of Statutory Interpretation*, 35 Akron L. Rev. 451 (2001–2002).

Joseph A. Grundfest & A.C. Pritchard, *Statutes with Multiple Personality Disorders: The Value of Ambiguity in Statutory Design and Interpretation*, 54 Stan. L. Rev. 627 (2002).

Richard L. Hasen, *Bad Legislative Intent*, 2006 Wis. L. Rev. 843.

Richard L. Hasen, *End of the Dialogue? Political Polarization, the Supreme Court, and Congress*, 86 S. Cal. L. Rev. 205 (2013).

Michael P. Healy, *Spurious Interpretation Redux: Mead and the Shrinking Domain of Statutory Ambiguity*, 54 Admin. L. Rev. 673 (2002).

Edward Heath, Essay, *How Federal Judges Use Legislative History*, 25 J. Legis. 95 (1999).

Michael Herz, *Purposivism and Institutional Competence in Statutory Interpretation*, 2009 Mich. St. L. Rev. 89.

Virginia A. Hettinger & Christopher Zorn, *Explaining the Incidence and Timing of Congressional Responses to the U.S. Supreme Court*, 30 Legis. Stud. Q. 5 (2005).

Olatunde Johnson, *The Story of Bob Jones University v. United States (1983): Race, Religion and Congress' Extraordinary Acquiesence*, in Statutory Interpretation Stories (William N. Eskridge, Jr., Philip P. Frickey & Elizabeth Garrett eds.) 126–63 (New York: Foundation Press, 2011).

John F. Manning, *Competing Presumptions About Statutory Coherence*, 74 Fordham L. Rev. 2009 (2006).

John F. Manning, Response, *Deriving Rules of Statutory Interpretation from the Constitution*, 101 Colum. L. Rev. 1648 (2001).

John F. Manning, *Putting Legislative History to a Vote: A Response to Professor Siegel*, 53 Vand. L. Rev. 1529 (2000).

John F. Manning, *Textualism and Legislative Intent*, 91 Va. L. Rev. 419 (2005).

John F. Manning, *Textualism and the Equity of the Statute*, 101 Colum. L. Rev. 1 (2001).

John F. Manning, *What Divides Textualists from Purposivists?*, 106 Colum. L. Rev. 70 (2006).

John F. Manning, *Justice Scalia and the Legislative Process*, 62 N.Y.U. Ann. Surv. Am. L. 33 (2006).

Jerry L. Mashaw, *Norms, Practices, and the Paradox of Deference: A Preliminary Inquiry into Agency Statutory Interpretation*, 57 Admin. L. Rev. 501 (2005).

Mathew D. McCubbins & Daniel B. Rodriguez, *What Is New in the New Statutory Interpretation? Introduction to* The Journal of Contemporary Legal Issues *Symposium*, 14 J. Contemp. Legal Issues 535 (2005).

Paul E. McGreal, *A Constitutional Defense of Legislative History*, 13 Wm. & Mary Bill Rts. J. 1267 (2005).

Thomas W. Merrill, *The Story of Chevron USA Inc. v. Natural Resources Defense Council, Inc. (1984): Sometimes Great Cases Are Made Not Born*, in Statutory Interpretation Stories (William N. Eskridge, Jr., Philip P. Frickey & Elizabeth Garrett eds.) 164–95 (New York: Foundation Press, 2011).

Jonathan T. Molot, *Reexamining* Marbury *in the Administrative State: A Structural and Institutional Defense of Judicial Power over Statutory Interpretation*, 96 Nw. U. L. Rev. 1239 (2002).

Jonathan T. Molot, *The Rise and Fall of Textualism*, 106 Colum. L. Rev. 1 (2006).

Morell E. Mullins, Sr., *Coming to Terms with Strict and Liberal Construction*, 64 Alb. L. Rev. 9 (2000).

John Copeland Nagle, *The Worst Statutory Interpretation Case in History*, 94 Nw. U. L. Rev. 1445 (2000) (reviewing William D. Popkin, Statutes in Court: The History and Theory of Statutory Interpretation (1999)).

Caleb Nelson, *A Response to Professor Manning*, 91 Va. L. Rev. 451 (2005).

Caleb Nelson, *Statutory Interpretation and Decision Theory*, 74 U. Chi. L. Rev. 329 (2007) (reviewing Adrian Vermeule, Judging Under Uncertainty: An Institutional Theory of Legal Interpretation (2006)).

Caleb Nelson, *What is Textualism?*, 91 Va. L. Rev. 347 (2005).

David Nimmer, *Appreciating Legislative History: The Sweet and Sour Spots of the DMCA's Commentary*, 23 Cardozo L. Rev. 909 (2002).

Lars Noah, *Divining Regulatory Intent: The Place for a "Legislative History" of Agency Rules*, 51 Hastings L.J. 255 (2000).

Victoria F. Nourse, *A Decision Theory of Statutory Interpretation: Legislative History by the Rules*, 122 Yale L.J. 70 (2012).

Victoria F. Nourse & Jane S. Schacter, *The Politics of Legislative Drafting: A Congressional Case Study*, 77 N.Y.U. L. Rev. 575 (2002).

Gary E. O'Connor, *Restatement (First) of Statutory Interpretation*, 7 N.Y.U. J. Legis. & Pub. Pol'y 333 (2004).

Nicholas R. Parrillo, *Leviathan and Interpretive Revolution: The Administrative State, the Judiciary, and the Rise of Legislative History, 1890–1950*, 123 Yale L.J. 266 (2013).

Bruce G. Peabody, *Congressional Constitutional Interpretation and the Courts: A Preliminary Inquiry into Legislative Attitudes, 1959–2001,* 29 Law & Soc. Inquiry 127 (2004).

Richard A. Posner, *Reply: The Institutional Dimension of Statutory and Constitutional Interpretation,* 101 Mich. L. Rev. 952 (2003).

Zachary Price, *The Rule of Lenity as a Rule of Structure,* 72 Fordham L. Rev. 885 (2004).

Todd D. Rakoff, *Statutory Interpretation as a Multifarious Enterprise,* 104 Nw. U. L. Rev. 1559 (2010).

John C. Roberts, *Are Congressional Committees Constitutional?: Radical Textualism, Separation of Powers, and the Enactment Process,* 52 Case W. Res. L. Rev. 489 (2001).

Daniel B. Rodriguez & Barry R. Weingast, *The Paradox of Expansionist Statutory Interpretations,* 101 Nw. U. L. Rev. 1207 (2007).

Daniel B. Rodriguez & Barry R. Weingast, *The Positive Political Theory of Legislative History: New Perspectives on the 1964 Civil Rights Act and Its Interpretation,* 151 U. Pa. L. Rev. 1417 (2003).

Nicholas Quinn Rosenkranz, *Federal Rules of Statutory Interpretation,* 115 Harv. L. Rev. 2085 (2002).

Edward Rubin, *Dynamic Statutory Interpretation in the Administrative State,* Issues in Legal Scholarship, bepress.com (2002).

Theodore W. Ruger, *The Story of FDA v. Brown & Williamson (2000): The Norm of Agency Continuity,* in Statutory Interpretation Stories (William N. Eskridge, Jr., Philip P. Frickey & Elizabeth Garrett eds.) 334–65 (New York: Foundation Press, 2011).

Jane S. Schacter, *The Confounding Common Law Originalism in Recent Supreme Court Statutory Interpretation: Implications for the Legislative History Debate and Beyond,* 51 Stan. L. Rev. 1 (1998).

Robert W. Scheef, *Temporal Dynamics in Statutory Interpretation: Courts, Congress, and the Canon of Constitutional Avoidance,* 64 U. Pitt. L. Rev. 529 (2003).

Charles E. Schumer, *Under Attack: Congressional Power in the Twenty-first Century,* 1 Harv. L & Pol'y Rev. 1 (2007).

Catherine M. Sharkey, *Inside Agency Preemption,* 110 Mich. L. Rev. 521 (2012).

Jonathan R. Siegel, *Timing and Delegation: A Reply,* 53 Vand. L. Rev. 1543 (2000).

Jonathan R. Siegel, *The Use of Legislative History in a System of Separated Powers,* 53 Vand. L. Rev. 1457 (2000).

Michael Sinclair, *The Proper Treatment of "Interpretive Choice" in Statutory Decision-Making,* 45 N.Y.L. Sch. L. Rev. 389 (2002).

Lawrence M. Solan, *Private Language, Public Laws: The Central Role of Legislative Intent in Statutory Interpretation,* 93 Geo. L.J. 427 (2005).

Kevin M. Stack, *Agency Statutory Interpretation and Policymaking Form,* 2009 Mich. St. L. Rev. 225.

Kevin M. Stack, *The Divergence of Constitutional and Statutory Interpretation*, 75 U. Colo. L. Rev. 1 (2004).

Nancy Staudt, Lee Epstein, Peter Wiedenbeck, René Lindstädt & Ryan J. Vander Wielen, *Judging Statutes: Interpretative Regimes*, 38 Loy. L.A. L. Rev. 1909 (2005).

Nancy C. Staudt, René Lindstädt & Jason O'Connor, *Judicial Decisions as Legislation: Congressional Oversight of Supreme Court Tax Cases, 1954–2005*, 82 N.Y.U. L. Rev. 1340 (2007).

Matthew C. Stephenson, *Legislative Allocation of Delegated Power: Uncertainty, Risk, and the Choice Between Agencies and Courts*, 119 Harv. L. Rev. 1035 (2006).

Peter L. Strauss, *The Courts and the Congress: Should Judges Disdain Political History?*, 98 Colum. L. Rev. 242 (1998).

Cass R. Sunstein & Adrian Vermeule, *Interpretation and Institutions*, 101 Mich. L. Rev. 885 (2003).

Cass R. Sunstein & Adrian Vermeule, *Interpretive Theory in Its Infancy: A Reply to Posner*, 101 Mich. L. Rev. 972 (2003).

Timothy P. Terrell, *Statutory Epistemology: Mapping the Interpretation Debate*, 53 Emory L.J. 523 (2004).

Charles Tiefer, *The Reconceptualization of Legislative History in the Supreme Court*, 2000 Wis. L. Rev. 205.

Adrian Vermeule, *The Cycles of Statutory Interpretation*, 68 U. Chi. L. Rev. 149 (2001).

Jeremy Waldron, *Legislating with Integrity*, 72 Fordham L. Rev. 373 (2003).

Abby Wright, Comment, *For All Intents and Purposes: What Collective Intention Tells Us About Congress and Statutory Interpretation*, 154 U. Pa. L. Rev. 983 (2006).

Ernest A. Young, *The Story of Gregory v. Ashcroft (1991): Clear Statement Rules and the Statutory Constitution of American Federalism*, in Statutory Interpretation Stories (William N. Eskridge, Jr., Philip P. Frickey & Elizabeth Garrett eds.) 196–225 (New York: Foundation Press, 2011).

ACKNOWLEDGMENTS

The occasion of the James Madison Lecture at New York University School of Law provided me an opportunity to offer ideas on the subject of statutes, ideas which I have further developed in this book. I was deeply honored to follow the many distinguished Supreme Court Justices and appellate judges who had been Madison Lecturers and am very grateful to Professor Norman Dorsen and then-Dean Richard Revesz for inviting me.

For this book, I give many thanks to many people. Adam Liptak first suggested that I consider expanding the Madison Lecture into a book. Then-Dean Revesz, Yale Law School Dean Robert Post, Judge Jay Harvie Wilkinson III, and Professor Ronald K.L. Collins were very helpful advisors about the book publication process. Professor James Brudney of Fordham Law School, editor Jennifer Callahan, Justice Gary Katzmann of the Massachusetts Appeals Court, and Russell Wheeler, the president of the Governance Institute and a Visiting Fellow of the Brookings Institution, were exceedingly generous in their careful review of the manuscript. I benefitted greatly from their insights. Michael Bosworth, Caleb Deats, Ilana Gelfman, Patrick Hughes, Amy Marshak, Lindsay Nash, William Perdue, Harker Rhodes, Brian Richardson, and Matthew Shahabian also provided very thoughtful comments about various chapters.

The Second Circuit's librarians, most especially Luis Lopez, Adriana Mark, Mark Schwartz, and Raymond Wong, were always expert in their assistance. At Oxford University Press, I was aided by an impressive team. With a keen sense of the big picture as well as close attention to detail, David McBride, Editor-in-Chief, Social Sciences, made many excellent suggestions that have made this work both more accessible and more precise; Sarah Rosenthal, Assistant Editor, was always a steady navigator throughout the publication process. Joellyn Ausanka and her production associates adhered to the highest standards. I remember well my meetings with Niko Pfund, President of Oxford University Press USA, who graciously took time from his busy schedule to talk to me about his extraordinary enterprise.

I count myself so fortunate to have learned so much from my great colleagues on the courts of the Second Circuit and in the federal judiciary more widely, including fellow members of the U.S. Judicial Conference Committee on the Judicial Branch as well as the able court executives and staff of the federal judiciary. How special it has been, and how thankful I am, to be part of the Third Branch, to develop meaningful friendships with my colleagues and their families. Throughout this book, I have referred to many judges and justices, who I deeply admire. I note with special appreciation two judges who are no longer with us, but who were unflagging boosters, Judge Frank M. Coffin and Judge Hugh H. Bownes. And there are these distinguished jurists who I came to know in my pre-bench days, and whose continuing kindness, encouragement, and generous friendship over many years I gratefully acknowledge: Ruth Bader Ginsburg (and Marty too), Stephen G. Breyer, and David H. Souter. I thank as well the many legislators and staffs of both parties, who I have known over the years, whose dedication to public service and the public good I so greatly respect. The continuing vitality of the project on statutory housekeeping owes much to the support of Senator Orrin Hatch, Senator Patrick Leahy, Senator Jeff Sessions, Representative John Conyers, Representative Lamar Smith, and Russell Wheeler.

Daniel P. Moynihan and James Q. Wilson taught me so much about political institutions and the former vigorously sponsored my judicial nomination. I consider myself lucky indeed to have had the continuing friendship of Elizabeth B. Moynihan, whom I met decades ago in the Moynihan home on Francis Avenue in Cambridge. I recall as well with warm thanks my colleagues at the Brookings Institution and Georgetown University. For nearly thirty years, I have savored my relationship with the Governance Institute, whose board members, officers and researchers have been extraordinary, both professionally and personally. The opportunity over the last decade to teach an administrative law seminar at the NYU School of Law, with thanks to Deans John Sexton, Revesz, and Trevor Morrison, has given me a chance to think about the issues in this book, apart from my own judicial experience. And for many years, I had the pleasure of co-teaching a one day program on statutory interpretation at the NYU School of Law Opperman Institute of Judicial Administration (IJA), with two brilliant masters of their craft, William Eskridge and Judge Diarmuid O'Scannlain—the former, the pathbreaking innovator of the modern field of legislation studies, and the latter, a renowned and highly-influential jurist. The energetic leadership of IJA—Oscar Chase, Samuel Estreicher, Troy McKenzie, and Torrey Whitman—has always been welcoming and I have always looked forward to participating in the annual program for new appellate judges.

With much appreciation, I note that I would not have had the opportunity to offer a judge's perspective on interpreting statutes had President Clinton not nominated me to the federal bench, at the urging of Senator Moynihan and with the aid of Gene Sperling. Nor would I have had that opportunity without Senate confirmation. In that regard, I remember the kindnesses of Senator Charles E. Schumer, who met with me before my nomination, and who offered generous words at my hearing, as well as the support of Senator Hatch and Senator Leahy, then chairman and ranking member of the Senate Judiciary Committee, respectively.

Apart from my Second Circuit judicial family, my judicial colleagues nationwide, and others already mentioned, over the years I have had the good fortune to have had enlightening and stimulating conversations about governmental institutions with so many astute individuals, including: Joel Aberbach, Allison Abner, Shirley Abrahamson, Alex Aleinikoff, Alan Altshuler, Anthony Arend, Richard Arnold, Michael Bailey, Veyom Bahl, Nina Bang-Jensen, Preeta Bansal, John Q. Barrett, Robert Bauer, Lawrence Baum, Vicki Been, M. Douglass Bellis, Walter Berns, John Bernstein, Marver Bernstein, Nina Bernstein, Sarah Binder, Diane Blair, Preet Bharara, Noel Brennan, Lawrence Brown, Anthony Bullock, William Burchill, Frank Burk, Sarah Burr, William Burton, Michael Breyer, Peter Byrne, Maureen Callahan, Colin Campbell, Michael Cardozo, Daniel Carpenter, Louis Casamayou, Maureen Casamayou, Steven Charnovitz, Mark Childress, Bruce Cohen, Stanley Cohen, Nadine Cohodas, Gregory Craig, Mariano-Florentino Cuéllar, Dan Cunningham, Michael Davidson, Nancy Davidson, Roger H. Davidson, Susan Davies, Charles Dellheim, Martha Derthick, Neal Devins, Matthew Diller, Viet Dinh, E.J. Dionne, Sam Dolnick, Suzanne Ducat, James Duff, Peter Eikenberry, Lawrence Evans, Jonathan Fanton, Judith Feder, Noah Feldman, Elizabeth Fine, Louis Fisher, Owen Fiss, Michael Fitts, Joel Fleishman, Christopher Foreman, John Fortier, James Fransen, Leon Fresco, Barry Friedman, David Frohnmayer, Michael Gellert, John Gilmour, Robert Giuffra, Abbe Gluck, Sheldon Goldman, William Gormley, Mary Graham, C. Boyden Gray, Kathryn Greenberg, Linda Greenhouse, Judah Gribetz, Laura Gross, Jacob Hacker, Caitlin Halligan, Mark Hamblett, Geoffrey Hathaway, Alice Henkin, Louis Henkin, Bert Huang, Richard Heffner, Paul Herrnson, Richard Hertling, Michael Herz, Beth Hess, Stephen Hess, Cynthia Hogan, Brock Hornby, Patricia Hynes, Richard Jaffe, Valerie Jarrett, Charles O. Jones, Susan Henshaw Jones, Robert Juceam, Elena Kagan, Jeffrey Kampelman, Max Kampelman, Robert W. Kastenmeier, Herbert Kaufman, Robert Kaufman, Ruth Kaufman, Judith Kaye, Cynthia Kelly, William C. Kelly Jr., John Kingdon, Laird Kirkpatrick, Ron Klain, Philip Klinkner, Lisa Kloppenberg, Harold Koh, Jessica Korn, Peter Kougasian, Larry Kramer, William Kristol, Jules Kroll, Lynn Kroll, John Kulewicz, Eric Lane, Esther Lardent, Martin Lederman, Christopher Leman, A. Leo Levin, Jacob Lew, Neil Lewis, Robert Lieber, Paul Light, Lewis Liman, Lisa Liman, Hans Linde, Jonathan Lippman, Seymour Martin Lipset, Robert Loesche, Jeffrey Lubbers, Kristine Lucius, Tamera Luzzato, Arthur Maass, Robert Mallett, Sheilah Mann, Thomas E. Mann, Forrest Maltzman, Peter Markowitz, Stephanie Martz, Jerry Mashaw, Tony Mauro, Calvin McKenzie, Francis J. McNamara Jr., Shep Melnick, Carol Messito, Gillian Metzger, Abner Mikva, Jeffrey Minear, Jonathan Mintz, Terry Moe, Robert Morgenthau, Alan Morrison, Phillip Mundo, Eusebio Mujal-Leon, Richard Nathan, Richard E. Neustadt, Pietro Nivola, Bernard Nussbaum, David O'Brien, Laurence O'Donnell, Lesley Oelsner, Michael O'Neill,

Norman Ornstein, Juan Osuna, Eric Patashnik, Mark Patterson, Paul Pierson, Robert Pitofsky, John Podesta, Julia Preston, Paul Quirk, Barry Rabe, Ann Rakoff, Douglas Reed, James Reichley, Michael Remington, Judith Resnik, Sally Rider, Roy Riordan, Bert Rockman, Daniel Rodriguez, Mark Rom, Albert Romano, Roberta Romano, Daniel Rose, Joanna Rose, Albert Rosenblatt, Edward Rubin, David Rudenstine, Timothy J. Russert, Kenneth Sagat, Stephanie Herseth Sandlin, Bryna Sanger, Charlie Savage, Wendy Schiller, Peter Schuck, Fritz Schwarz, Jeffrey A. Segal, Betsy Seidman, Harold Seidman, David Sellers, Kirk Semple, George Shambaugh, Stephen Shannon, Martin Shapiro, Kevin Sheekey, Jeff Shesol, Charles Shipan, John Siffert, Andrew Sigler, Sylvan Sobel, Steven Solomon, Gene Sperling, Andrew Stark, Janet Steiger, Gilbert Steiner, Mark Steinmeyer, Richard Stewart, Peter Strauss, Cordia Strom, Herbert Sturz, Thomas Sugrue, Kathleen Sullivan, James L. Sundquist, Bruce Swartz, Deanell Tacha, Strobe Talbott, Kathryn Dunn Tenpas, Steven Tevlowitz, James Thurber, Charles Tiefer, John Tierney, Rachel Tiven, Allison Treanor, William Treanor, Barbara Underwood, Donna Verdier, Stephen Verdier, Paul Verkuil, David Vladeck, Paul Volcker, Michael Waldman, Stephen Wasby, Stephen Wayne, Kent Weaver, Eric Weingartner, Robert Weisel, Darrell West, Alan Westin, Joseph White, Shelby White, Sarah Wilson, Deborah Winshel, Ben Wittes, Frank Wohl, David Yalof, John Yoo, Kenji Yoshino, William Zabel, Mark Zauderer, and Julian Zelizer. Thanks to C-Span and Brian Lamb, it is possible to observe government in action, even from my home base of New York.

I cannot adequately say in words what a privilege and joy it has been to know and work with my wonderful law clerks. My judicial assistant from my first day on the bench, Dominique Welch, has been simply superb. I look forward each day to the challenges ahead because of my colleagues in chambers, and am so thankful for the friendships that thrive beyond the clerkship experience.

Finally, a special word of profound appreciation to my family, whose steadfast support has made all the difference and made everything possible for me—my parents, John and Sylvia Katzmann, and my siblings, Gary, Martin and Susan, and their families. Sonia Sotomayor has been an always caring sister to me. I dedicate this book to my spouse, Jennifer, who, apart from her insightful suggestions about the preceding chapters, and her constant understanding and encouragement, has given my life so much happiness, enriching it in so many ways.

NOTES

Preface

1. *See generally* ROBERT A. KATZMANN, REGULATORY BUREAUCRACY: THE FED-
    ERAL TRADE COMMISSION AND ANTITRUST POLICY (1980).
2. *See generally* ROBERT A. KATZMANN, INSTITUTIONAL DISABILITY: THE SAGA
    OF TRANSPORTATION POLICY FOR THE DISABLED (1986) (examining how leg-
    islative, administrative, and judicial processes have dealt with problems of mo-
    bility for the disabled).
3. Created in 1986, the Governance Institute is a small nonprofit organization
    in Washington, D.C., concerned with exploring, explaining, and easing prob-
    lems associated with both the separation and the division of powers in the
    American federal system. The Institute's focus is on institutional process—a
    nexus linking law, institutions, and policy. Products of the Governance Insti-
    tute's program on judicial-legislative relations include: ROBERT A. KATZMANN,
    COURTS AND CONGRESS (1997) [hereinafter KATZMANN, COURTS AND
    CONGRESS]; JUDGES AND LEGISLATORS: TOWARD INSTITUTIONAL COMITY
    (Robert A. Katzmann ed., 1988) [hereinafter JUDGES AND LEGISLATORS];
    Frank M. Coffin, *Communication Among the Three Branches: Can the Bar Serve as
    Catalyst?*, 75 JUDICATURE 125 (1991); Frank M. Coffin & Robert A. Katzmann,
    Steps Towards Optimal Judicial Workways: Perspectives from the Federal Bench,
    59 N.Y.U. ANN. SURV. AM. L. 377 (2003); Robert A. Katzmann & Russell
    R. Wheeler, *A Mechanism for "Statutory Housekeeping": Appellate Courts Working
    with Congress*, 9 J. APP. PRAC. & PROCESS 131 (2007); Robert A. Katzmann &
    Russell R. Wheeler, *A Primer on Interbranch Relations*, 95 GEO. L.J. 1155 (2007).
    Russell Wheeler is currently the president of the Governance Institute.

4. JUDGES AND LEGISLATORS, *supra* note 3, at vii.
5. KATZMANN, COURTS AND CONGRESS, *supra* note 3 (examining "key aspects of the relationship between the courts and Congress," including "the confirmation process, communications, statutory interpretation, and statutory revision").

Chapter 1

1. In the Supreme Court Terms 2010–2012, nearly two-thirds of the cases involved pure statutory (43.28 percent) and mixed statutory/constitutional cases (19.75 percent), and only a little more than a quarter of the cases (27.31 percent) involved pure constitutional cases. E-mail from Matthew Shahabian, on compilation done by Shahabian, Caleb Deats, Ilana Gelfman, and Patrick Hughes, to author (Aug. 1, 2013, 11:41 AM EST) (on file with author). William Eskridge, Jr. estimates that in 2008, two-thirds of the Supreme Court's caseload consisted of pure statutory cases, and just one-fourth consisted of pure constitutional cases. E-mail from William N. Eskridge, Jr., John A. Garver Professor of Jurisprudence, Yale Law School, to author (Aug. 8, 2011, 10:12 AM EST) (on file with author).
2. Nat'l Fed'n of Indep. Bus. v. Sebelius, 132 S. Ct. 2566 (2012) (upholding in part the Patient Protection and Affordable Care Act, Pub. L. No. 111-148, 124 Stat. 119 (2010)).
3. 21 U.S.C. § 844 (2006).
4. *See* United States v. Morgan, 412 F. App'x 357, 359–60 (2d Cir. 2011) (rejecting appellant's claim that his purchase of pseudoephedrine for personal consumption did not violate the statute because Congress's purpose, on his argument, was to prevent the manufacture of methamphetamine).
5. Murphy v. Arlington Cent. Sch. Dist. Bd. of Educ., 402 F.3d 332 (2d Cir. 2005) (holding that expert fees are compensable costs under the statute), *rev'd*, 548 U.S. 291 (2006).
6. 20 U.S.C. § 1415(i)(3)(B) (2006) (emphasis added).
7. 28 U.S.C. § 2680(b) (2006) (emphasis added).
8. *See* Raila v. United States, 355 F.3d 118 (2d Cir. 2004) (holding that the plaintiff's claims under the Federal Tort Claims Act were not barred by the statute's postal matter exception); Dolan v. U.S. Postal Serv., 546 U.S. 481 (2006) (upholding *Raila*).
9. 18 U.S.C. § 922 (emphasis added).
10. *See* United States v. Gayle, 342 F.3d 89 (2d Cir. 2003) (holding that convictions in foreign courts did not satisfy the "convicted in any court" element of the statute (quoting 18 U.S.C. § 922 (2006))); *see also* United States v. Small, 544 U.S. 385 (2004) (upholding *Gayle*).
11. *See Statutory Interpretation and the Uses of Legislative History: Hearing Before the Subcomm. on Courts, Intellectual Prop., and the Admin. of Justice of the H. Comm.*

on the Judiciary, 101st Cong. (1990); *see also Interbranch Relations: Hearings Before the Joint Comm. on the Org. of Cong.*, 103d Cong. 76, 298 (1993).

12. *See infra* text accompanying ch. 4, nn. 28–29 (noting Senator Grassley's questions at confirmation hearings); *id.* at n.32 (Senator Franken urging nominee Elena Kagan to consider legislative history).

13. *See infra* App. B (noting publications on statutory interpretation over the last fifteen years).

14. Pub. L. No. 111-2, 123 Stat. 5 (to be codified at 42 U.S.C. § 2000e-5).

15. *See, e.g.*, Gail Collins, Op-Ed., *Lilly's Big Day*, N.Y. TIMES, Jan. 29, 2009, at A27; Sheryl Gay Stolberg, *Obama Signs Equal-Pay Legislation*, N.Y. TIMES, Jan. 29, 2009, http://www.nytimes.com/2009/01/30/us/politics/30ledbetter-web.html.

16. 550 U.S. 618, 661 (2007) (Ginsburg, J., dissenting) ("As in 1991, the Legislature may act to correct this Court's parsimonious reading of Title VII.").

17. Pub. L. No. 88-352, 78 Stat. 241, 253 (codified as amended at 42 U.S.C. § 2000e *et seq.* (2006)).

18. *Ledbetter*, 550 U.S. at 661 (Ginsburg, J., dissenting).

19. *See, e.g.*, Robert Barnes, *Supreme Court Lawyers Cautious When Offering One Specific Piece of Evidence*, WASH. POST, Apr. 22, 2012, http://articles.washingtonpost.com/2012-04-22/politics/35452738_1_justice-sonia-sotomayor-legislative-history-lawyers-offer.

20. Rick Richman, *Scalia, Sotomayor Light Up High Court Hearing on Arizona Voting Rights Case*, Mar. 20, 2013, http://www.nysun.com/national/scalia-sotomayor-light-up-high-court-hearing/88232/.

21. Richman, *Scalia, Sotomayor, supra* note 20.

22. Richman, *Scalia, Sotomayor, supra* note 20.

23. *Key Moments from the Hearing on the Defense of Marriage Act*, N.Y. TIMES, Mar. 27, 2013, http://www.nytimes.com/interactive/2013/03/27/us/supreme-court-defense-of-marriage-act.html?_r=0 (quoting H.R. REP. No. 104-664, at 15–16 (1996)).

24. 5 U.S. (1 Cranch) 137 (1803); *see* MARK TUSHNET, ARGUING MARBURY V. MADISON (2005) (presenting historical background and analysis of *Marbury* scholarship); William Michael Treanor, *The Story of* Marbury v. Madison: *Judicial Autonomy and Political Struggle, in* FEDERAL COURTS STORIES 29–56 (Vicki C. Jackson & Judith Resnik eds., 2010).

25. Charles O. Jones, *A Way of Life and Law*, 89 AM. POL. SCI. REV. 1, 8 (1995).

26. *See, e.g.*, Federal Trade Commission Act of 1914, 15 U.S.C. § 45(a) (2006) (establishing requirements designed to prevent "unfair or deceptive acts or practices in or affecting commerce").

27. *See, e.g.*, 42 U.S.C. § 2000e-2 (proscribing discrimination on the basis of race, color, religion, sex, or national origin); Americans with Disabilities Act of 1990, 42 U.S.C. § 12112 (2006) (proscribing discrimination on the basis of disability).

28. *See,* e.g., Federal Water Pollution Control Act Amendments of 1972 ("Clean Water Act"), 33 U.S.C. §§ 1251–52, 1362(7) (2006) (prohibiting the discharge of any pollutant into "navigable waters," defined without further elaboration as "the waters of the United States, including the territorial seas").

29. *See,* e.g., 23 U.S.C. § 158(a) (2006) (directing the Secretary of Transportation to withhold a percentage of federal highway funds otherwise allocable from States "in which the purchase or public possession... of any alcoholic beverage by a person who is less than twenty-one years of age is lawful"); South Dakota v. Dole, 483 U.S. 203, 211–12 (1987) (holding that 23 U.S.C. § 158 was a valid exercise of Congress's spending power).

30. *See,* e.g., Balanced Budget and Emergency Deficit Control Act of 1985 ("Gramm-Rudman-Hollings Act"), 2 U.S.C. § 922 (2006) (authorizing members of Congress to file a suit challenging the constitutionality of the Act and providing for challenge to be heard by a special three-judge federal court with direct appeal to the Supreme Court); *see generally* CHARLES R. SHIPAN, DESIGNING JUDICIAL REVIEW 97–121 (1999) (examining legislative provisions for judicial review).

31. *See* Robert A. Katzmann, *The American Legislative Process as a Signal,* 9 J. PUB. POL'Y 287, 292 (1989) ("As a signal of government, legislation affects both the substance and process of policymaking."); *see also* Michael Herz, *Judicial Textualism Meets Congressional Micromanagement: A Potential Collision in Clear Air Act Interpretation,* 16 HARV. ENVTL. L. REV. 175, 180 (1992) (noting Congress's tendency to micromanage environmental agencies through extremely detailed legislation).

32. On the impact of statutes on the administrative state in the twentieth century, see JAMES WILLARD HURST, THE GROWTH OF AMERICAN LAW 419–23 (1950), where the author explains that the "sheer bulk" of legislation and the need for expertise drove the creation of specialized agencies in the years after 1910. *See also* JAMES WILLARD HURST, DEALING WITH STATUTES (1982); CASS R. SUNSTEIN, AFTER THE RIGHTS REVOLUTION: RECONCEIVING THE REGULATORY STATE (1990). Grant Gilmore famously described the "orgy of statute making" in GRANT GILMORE, THE AGES OF AMERICAN LAW 95 (1977).

33. Pub. L. No. 79-404, 60 Stat. 237 (1946) (codified as amended in scattered sections of 5 U.S.C.).

34. Pub. L. No. 101-336, 104 Stat. 327 (codified as amended at 42 U.S.C. §§ 12, 101–213 (2006)).

35. Pub. L. No. 88-206, 77 Stat. 392 (1963) (codified as amended at 42 U.S.C. §§ 7401 *et seq.* (2006)).

36. The "Clean Water Act" was at first called the Federal Water Pollution Control Act Amendments, Pub. L. No. 92-500, 86 Stat. 816 (1972) (codified as amended at 33 U.S.C. §§ 1251 *et seq.* (2006)).

37. Pub. L. No. 92-318, 86 Stat. 235 (codified as amended at 20 U.S.C. §§ 1681 *et seq.* (2006)).

38. Barbara Winslow, *The Impact of Title IX*, THE GILDER LEHRMAN INST. OF AM. HISTORY, http://www.gilderlehrman.org/history-by-era/seventies/essays/impact-title-ix (last visited Oct. 4, 2013) (noting that Title IX is "[o]ne of the great achievements of the women's movement" and that its impact extends beyond sports to higher education, employment, learning environment, math and science, sexual harassment, standardized testing, and technology). For more information on Title IX's impact on education, see generally KATHERINE HANSON, VIVIAN GUILFOY & SARITA PILLAI, MORE THAN TITLE IX: HOW EQUITY IN EDUCATION HAS SHAPED THE NATION (2009), where the author examines the broader societal changes that followed Title IX and its focus on gender equity in education.

39. WILLIAM N. ESKRIDGE JR. & JOHN FEREJOHN, A REPUBLIC OF STATUTES: THE NEW AMERICAN CONSTITUTION (2010); *see also* DAVID R. MAYHEW, DIVIDED WE GOVERN: PARTY CONTROL, LAWMAKING, AND INVESTIGATIONS, 1946–2002, at 4 (2d ed. 2005) (arguing that whether Congress is unified or divided has made little difference in the incidence of highly publicized congressional investigations or important legislation); Forrest Maltzman & Charles R. Shipan, *Change, Continuity, and the Evolution of the Law*, 52 AM. J. POL. SCI. 252 (2008) (examining the political conditions that influence whether a law comes under review or is changed in subsequent years).

40. 347 U.S. 483 (1954).

41. Pub. L. No. 88-352, 78 Stat. 241 (1964) (codified as amended at 42 U.S.C. § 2000e *et seq.* (2006)).

42. *See, e.g.*, Thompson v. N. Am. Stainless, LP, 131 S. Ct. 863 (2011) (holding that an employee who claims he was terminated because his fiancée had filed a discrimination charge against their mutual employer may pursue a retaliation claim under Title VII); Jones v. Alfred H. Mayer Co., 392 U.S. 409, 438–39 (1968) (holding that 42 U.S.C. § 1982 prohibits racial discrimination in housing by private, as well as governmental, housing providers).

43. *See, e.g.*, Wilner v. Nat'l Sec. Agency, 592 F.3d 60, 74–75 (2d Cir. 2009) (upholding, under section 6 of the National Security Agency Act of 1959, 50 U.S.C. § 402 (2006), a denial of a request under the Freedom of Information Act, 5 U.S.C. § 552 (2006), for information gathered under the Terrorist Surveillance Program, because the requested information would reveal activities of the National Security Agency).

44. *See, e.g.*, Massachusetts v. EPA, 549 U.S. 497, 532 (2007) (holding that section 202(a)(1) of the Clean Air Act, 42 U.S.C. § 7521(a)(1) (2006), gives the Environmental Protection Agency authority to regulate emissions of greenhouse gases from new motor vehicles).

45. *See, e.g.*, Morrison v. Nat'l Austl. Bank Ltd., 130 S. Ct. 2869, 2888 (2010) (holding that section 10(b) of the Securities Exchange Act of 1934, 15 U.S.C. § 78j(b) (2006), does not provide a cause of action to foreign plaintiffs suing foreign and American defendants for misconduct in connection with securities traded on foreign exchanges).

46. *See,* e.g., Bartlett v. Strickland, 556 U.S. 1, 14–15 (2009) (holding that a racial minority group that constitutes less than fifty percent of a proposed district's population cannot state a vote dilution claim under section 2 of the Voting Rights Act of 1965, 42 U.S.C. § 1973 (2006)).

47. *See,* e.g., Meritor Sav. Bank v. Vinson, 477 U.S. 57, 66 (1986) (holding that a plaintiff could establish a violation of Title VII "by proving that discrimination based on sex has created a hostile or abusive work environment").

48. Guido Calabresi, A Common Law for the Age of Statutes 1 (Cambridge, MA: Harvard University Press, 1982) (arguing that "many disparate current legal-political phenomena are reactions" to the fundamental change of American law from a legal system once dominated by common law to a system dominated by statutes); *see also* Judith S. Kaye, *State Courts at the Dawn of a New Century: Common Law Courts Reading Statutes and Constitutions,* 70 N.Y.U. L. Rev. 1 (1995) (discussing the role of state judges in interpreting state statutes and constitutions). *See generally* Abbe R. Gluck, *The States as Laboratories of Statutory Interpretation: Methodological Consensus and the New Modified Textualism,* 119 Yale L.J. 1750 (2010).

49. State court cases interpreting statutes are numerous. *See,* e.g., Commonwealth v. Gomez, 940 N.E.2d 488, 492–93 (Mass. App. Ct. 2011) (explaining that statutes on the same subject matter should be read as a whole to produce internal consistency); Gordon v. Registry of Motor Vehicles, 912 N.E.2d 9, 13 (Mass. App. Ct. 2009) (determining that whether a statute is criminal or civil depends on the legislature's intent, which is a matter of statutory construction); Samiento v. World Yacht Inc., 883 N.E.2d 990, 993–94 (N.Y. 2008) (employing a purposivist technique); Kramer v. Zoning Bd. of Appeals, 837 N.E.2d 1147, 1152 (Mass. App. Ct. 2005) ("[S]tatutes are to be interpreted in a common-sense way which is consistent with the statutory scheme, and in a way which avoids constitutional issues."); State v. Courchesne, 816 A.2d 562, 578 (Conn. 2003) (explaining that statute should be interpreted in consideration of "all of those sources beyond the language itself, without first having to cross any threshold of ambiguity of the language").

50. Stephen Breyer, Making Our Democracy Work 102 (New York: Alfred A. Knopf, 2010).

Chapter 2

1. Daniel Patrick Moynihan, Came the Revolution: Argument in the Reagan Era 66 (1988).

2. Moynihan, *supra* note 1.

3. The Federalist No. 62, at 445 (James Madison) (Pocket Books ed., 2004).

4. The Federalist No. 63, *supra* note 3, at 451 (James Madison).

5. *See* THE FEDERALIST NO. 53, *supra* note 3, at 388 (James Madison) ("The greater the proportion of new members, and the less the information of the bulk of the members, the more apt will they be to fall into the snares that may be laid for them.").

6. THE FEDERALIST NO. 62, *supra* note 3, at 447 (James Madison).

7. U.S. CONST. art. I § 2, cl. 6.

8. U.S. CONST. art. I § 3, cl. 4.

9. U.S. CONST. art. I § 5, cl. 2.

10. U.S. CONST. art. I § 5, cl. 3.

11. U.S. CONST. art. I § 5, cl. 4.

12. U.S. CONST. art. I § 7, cl. 1.

13. U.S. CONST. art. I § 6, cl. 1.

14. JAMES L. SUNDQUIST, CONSTITUTIONAL REFORM AND EFFECTIVE GOVERNMENT 1 (1986) (quoting Letter from Gouverneur Morris to W. H. Wells (Feb. 24, 1815), *in* 3 THE RECORDS OF THE FEDERAL CONVENTION OF 1787, at 421–22 (Max Farrand ed., rev. ed. 1937)).

15. *House History: 1st Congress (1789–1791)*, OFF. CLERK U.S. HOUSE REPRESENTATIVES, http://history.house.gov/Congressional-Overview/Profiles/ 1st/(last visited Oct. 4, 2013) (noting the number of members in the first House of Representatives); *The Senate Moves to Philadelphia*, U.S. SENATE, http://www.senate.gov/artandhistory/history/minute/The_Senate_Moves_ To_Philadelphia.htm (last visited Oct. 4, 2013) (noting the number of members in the first Senate).

16. *See* JOSEPH COOPER, THE ORIGINS OF THE STANDING COMMITTEES AND THE DEVELOPMENT OF THE MODERN HOUSE (1970) (analyzing the impact of the standing committee system in the House of Representatives); David T. Canon & Charles Stewart III, *The Evolution of the Committee System in Congress*, *in* CONGRESS RECONSIDERED 163 (Lawrence C. Dodd & Bruce I. Oppenheimer eds., 7th ed. 2001) (presenting evidence on the influence of select committees in the nineteenth century); Jeffery A. Jenkins & Charles H. Stewart III, *Order from Chaos: The Transformation of the Committee System in the House, 1816–1922*, *in* PARTY, PROCESS, AND POLITICAL CHANGE IN CONGRESS 195 (David W. Brady & Mathew D. McCubbins eds., 2002) (examining the social choice problems that contributed to the rise of the early nineteenth-century committee system); Eric Schickler, *Institutional Development of Congress*, *in* THE LEGISLATIVE BRANCH 35, 37–41 (Paul J. Quirk & Sarah A. Binder eds., 2005) (explaining the rise of the standing committee system in both the House of Representatives and the Senate); Gerald Gamm & Kenneth A. Shepsle, *Emergence of Legislative Institutions: Standing Committees in the House and Senate, 1810–1825*, 14 LEGIS. STUD. Q. 39, 39 (1989) (discussing and applying institutional development theories to the development of standing committees in Congress). On the study of the modern committee system and changes in

modern scholarship on committees, see C. Lawrence Evans, *Congressional Committees, in* THE OXFORD HANDBOOK OF THE AMERICAN CONGRESS 396 (Eric Schickler & Frances E. Lee eds., 2011).

17. WOODROW WILSON, CONGRESSIONAL GOVERNMENT 79 (15th prtg. 1901).

18. *See* RICHARD F. FENNO, JR., CONGRESSMEN IN COMMITTEES xiv–xv (1973).

19. David E. Price, *Legislative Ethics in the New Congress, in* REPRESENTATION AND RESPONSIBILITY: EXPLORING LEGISLATIVE ETHICS 129, 144 (Bruce Jennings & Daniel Callahan eds., 1985).

20. NORMAN J. ORNSTEIN, THOMAS E. MANN & MICHAEL J. MALBIN VITAL STATISTICS ON CONGRESS 2008, at 109–21 (2008); *see also* ROGER H. DAVIDSON, WALTER J. OLESZEK & FRANCES E. LEE, CONGRESS AND ITS MEMBERS 204–05 (13th ed. 2012) (discussing the influence and importance of committee staff in drafting, negotiating, and shaping legislation).

21. NORMAN J. ORNSTEIN, THOMAS E. MANN, MICHAEL J. MALBIN & ANDREW RUGG, VITAL STATISTICS ON CONGRESS 2013 tbl.4–6 (2013). [hereinafter ORNSTEIN ET AL., STATISTICS 2013], *available at* http://www.brookings.edu/research/reports/2013/07/vital-statistics-congress-mann-ornstein. Here, "committees" include standing committees, subcommittees of standing committees, select and special committees, subcommittees of select and special committees, joint committees, and subcommittees of joint committees. ORNSTEIN ET AL., STATISTICS 2013.

22. Roger H. Davidson, *The House of Representatives: Managing Legislative Complexity, in* WORKWAYS OF GOVERNANCE: MONITORING OUR GOVERNMENT'S HEALTH 24, 33 (Roger H. Davidson ed., 2003).

23. DONALD R. WOLFENSBERGER, BIPARTISAN POLICY CTR., A BRIEF HISTORY OF CONGRESSIONAL REFORM EFFORTS (2013), *available at* http://bipartisan-policy.org/library/democracy-project/brief-history-congressional-reform-efforts; ROGER H. DAVIDSON & WALTER J. OLESZEK, CONGRESS AGAINST ITSELF (1977); C. LAWRENCE EVANS & WALTER J. OLESZEK, CONGRESS UNDER FIRE: REFORM POLITICS AND THE REPUBLICAN MAJORITY (1997); Walter Kravitz, *The Advent of the Modern Congress: The Legislative Reorganization Act of 1970*, 15 LEGIS. STUD. Q. 375 (1990).

24. *Interbranch Relations: Hearings Before the Joint Comm. on the Org. of Cong.*, 103d Cong. 86, 298 (1993).

25. Frank M. Coffin, *Working with the Congress of the Future, in* THE FEDERAL APPELLATE JUDICIARY IN THE TWENTY-FIRST CENTURY 199, 202 (Cynthia Harrison & Russell R. Wheeler eds., 1989).

26. THOMAS E. MANN & NORMAN J. ORNSTEIN, IT'S EVEN WORSE THAN IT LOOKS (2013); Olympia J. Snowe, Op-Ed., *Why I am Leaving the Senate*, WASH. POST (Mar. 1, 2012), http://articles.washingtonpost.com/2012-03-01/opinions/35450357_1_senate-common-ground-olympia-snowe/; SARAH A. BINDER, STALEMATE: CAUSES AND CONSEQUENCES OF LEGISLATIVE GRIDLOCK (2003); Steven M. Teles, *Kludgeocracy in America*, 17 NAT'L AFF. 97 (2013).

27. *See generally* WALTER J. OLESZEK, CONGRESSIONAL PROCEDURES AND THE POLICY PROCESS 28 (8th ed. 2010) (discussing the congressional lawmaking process and how Congress's rules and procedures affect policy). For case studies of the legislative process, see the following sources: BRUCE A. ACKERMAN & WILLIAM T. HASSLER, CLEAN COAL/DIRTY AIR 26–58 (1981) (discussing the process of amending the Clean Air Act); PAUL C. LIGHT, FORGING LEGISLATION 169–71 (1991) (describing the approval of the Department of Veterans Affairs Act); ROBERT A. KATZMANN, INSTITUTIONAL DISABILITY: THE SAGA OF TRANSPORTATION POLICY FOR THE DISABLED 15–78 (1986) (describing disjointed congressional efforts to enhance mobility for the disabled in the 1970s); PHILIP G. SCHRAG, A WELL-FOUNDED FEAR: THE CONGRESSIONAL BATTLE TO SAVE POLITICAL ASYLUM IN AMERICA (1999) (charting an effort to restrict political asylum in the 104th Congress).

28. ORNSTEIN ET AL., STATISTICS 2013, *supra* note 21.

29. ORNSTEIN ET AL., STATISTICS 2013, *supra* note 21, at tbl.6-4.

30. ORNSTEIN ET AL., STATISTICS 2013, *supra* note 21, at tbl.6-1.

31. ORNSTEIN ET AL., STATISTICS 2013, *supra* note 21, at tbl.6-2.

32. ORNSTEIN ET AL., STATISTICS 2013, *supra* note 21.

33. These data were drawn from the Federal Register, Previous Sessions: Public Law Numbers, http://www.archives.gov/federal-register/laws/past/ (last visited Oct. 4, 2013).

34. ORNSTEIN ET AL., STATISTICS 2013, *supra* note 21, at tbl.6-1.

35. ORNSTEIN ET AL., STATISTICS 2013, *supra* note 21, at tbl.6-2.

36. DAVIDSON ET AL., CONGRESS AND ITS MEMBERS, *supra* note 20, at 172.

37. DAVIDSON ET AL., CONGRESS AND ITS MEMBERS, *supra* note 20, at 219 (noting that omnibus bills "contain an array of issues that were once handled as separate pieces of legislation").

38. DAVIDSON ET AL., CONGRESS AND ITS MEMBERS, *supra* note 20, at 221 (noting that omnibus bills "minimize the opportunities for further delay").

39. *See* ROGER H. DAVIDSON, WALTER J. OLESZEK & FRANCES E. LEE, CONGRESS AND ITS MEMBERS 241 (12th ed. 2009) (quoting a former chair of the House Budget Committee as saying that "[l]arge bills can be used to hide legislation that otherwise might be controversial").

40. David Brady & Morris Fiorina, *Congress in the Era of the Permanent Campaign, in* THE PERMANENT CAMPAIGN AND ITS FUTURE 134 (Norman J. Ornstein & Thomas E. Mann eds., 2000).

41. ORNSTEIN ET AL., STATISTICS 2013, *supra* note 21, at tbl.6-3.

42. ORNSTEIN ET AL., STATISTICS 2013, *supra* note 21.

43. ORNSTEIN ET AL., STATISTICS 2013, *supra* note 21.

44. ORNSTEIN ET AL., STATISTICS 2013, *supra* note 21.

45. ORNSTEIN ET AL., STATISTICS 2013, *supra* note 21.

46. ORNSTEIN ET AL., STATISTICS 2013, *supra* note 21.

47. ORNSTEIN ET AL., STATISTICS 2013, *supra* note 21, at tbl.6-1, tbl.6-2.

48. ORNSTEIN ET AL., STATISTICS 2013, *supra* note 21, at tbl.6-1.
49. ORNSTEIN ET AL., STATISTICS 2013, *supra* note 21.
50. ORNSTEIN ET AL., STATISTICS 2013, *supra* note 21, at tbl.6-2.
51. ORNSTEIN ET AL., STATISTICS 2013, *supra* note 21.
52. ORNSTEIN ET AL., STATISTICS 2013, *supra* note 21, at tbl.4-4.
53. ORNSTEIN ET AL., STATISTICS 2013, *supra* note 21.
54. ORNSTEIN ET AL., STATISTICS 2013, *supra* note 21, at tbl.4-5.
55. ORNSTEIN ET AL., STATISTICS 2013, *supra* note 21.
56. For a discussion on the challenges of deliberation, see generally SARAH A. BINDER, STALEMATE: CAUSES AND CONSEQUENCES OF LEGISLATIVE GRIDLOCK (2003); PAUL J. QUIRK & GARY MUCCIARONI, DELIBERATIVE CHOICES: DEBATING PUBLIC POLICY IN CONGRESS (2006).
57. For theoretical analyses of the congressional committee system, see, for example, KEITH KREHBIEL, INFORMATION AND LEGISLATIVE ORGANIZATION (1992); David P. Baron, *Legislative Organization with Informational Committees*, 44 AM. J. POL. SCI. 485 (2000); Thomas W. Gilligan & Keith Krehbiel, *Organization of Informative Committees by a Rational Legislature*, 34 AM. J. POL. SCI. 531 (1990); Forrest Maltzman, *Meeting Competing Demands: Committee Performance in the Postreform House*, 39 AM. J. POL. SCI. 653 (1995).
58. Collectible Coin Protection Act, H.R. 2754, 113th Cong. § 2 (2013).
59. James L. Buckley, a former senator from New York and judge on the D.C. Circuit, remarked that, as a senator, "My understanding of most of the legislation I voted on was based entirely on my reading of its language and, where necessary, on explanations contained in the accompanying report." *Statutory Interpretation and the Uses of Legislative History: Hearing Before the Subcomm. on Courts, Intellectual Prop., and the Admin. of Justice of the H. Comm. on the Judiciary*, 101st Cong. 21 (1990) (statement of James L. Buckley, J., D.C. Cir.). In the words of another former legislator and judge, Abner J. Mikva, a committee report is "the most useful document in the legislative history." Robert A. Katzmann, *Summary of Proceedings, in* JUDGES AND LEGISLATORS: TOWARD INSTITUTIONAL COMITY 162, 171 (Robert A. Katzmann ed., 1988).
60. James J. Brudney, *Canon Shortfalls and the Virtues of Political Branch Interpretive Assets*, 98 CALIF. L. REV. 1199, 1219–20 (2010); DONALD A. RITCHIE, PRESS GALLERY: CONGRESS AND THE WASHINGTON CORRESPONDENTS (1991); 2 ROBERT C. BYRD, THE SENATE 311–12 (1991); MILDRED AMER, CONG. RESEARCH SERV., CRS Report 93-60, THE CONGRESSIONAL RECORD; CONTENT, HISTORY AND ISSUES 1 (1993).
61. Brudney, *supra* note 60, at 1222; Thomas F. Broden, Jr., *Congressional Committee Reports: Their Role and History*, 33 NOTRE DAME L. REV. 209, 226–30 (1958); WILLIAM HOLMES BROWN & CHARLES JOHNSON, HOUSE PRACTICE 281 (2003); JAMES BRYCE, THE AMERICAN COMMONWEALTH 148, 155–57 (1891).
62. ANDREA LaRUE, SENATE MANUAL CONTAINING THE STANDING RULES, ORDERS, LAWS, AND RESOLUTIONS AFFECTING THE BUSINESS OF THE

UNITED STATES SENATE, S. DOC. NO. 107-1, at 17 (2001). This period of two days does not include Sundays and legal holidays. LARUE, SENATE MANUAL; *see also* JOHN V. SULLIVAN, CONSTITUTION, JEFFERSON'S MANUAL, AND RULES OF THE HOUSE OF REPRESENTATIVES, H.R. DOC. NO. 108-241, at 623 (2004).

63. *See,* e.g., GEORGE MILLER, LILLY LEDBETTER FAIR PAY ACT OF 2007, H.R. REP. NO. 110-237 (2007).
64. *See,* e.g., DON YOUNG, SAFE, ACCOUNTABLE, FLEXIBLE, EFFICIENT TRANSPORTATION ACT: A LEGACY FOR USERS, H.R. REP. NO. 109-105 (2005) (Conf. Rep.).
65. Clyde Wilcox, *The Dynamics of Lobbying the Hill, in* 1 THE INTEREST GROUP CONNECTION: ELECTIONEERING, LOBBYING, AND POLICYMAKING IN WASHINGTON 89 (Paul S. Herrnson, Ronald G. Shaiko & Clyde Wilcox eds., 1998) (noting that members of Congress are interested in obtaining views of interest groups on proposed legislation).
66. EDWARD M. KENNEDY, TRUE COMPASS 486 (2009).
67. ROBERT G. KAISER, ACT OF CONGRESS: HOW AMERICA'S ESSENTIAL INSTITUTION WORKS, AND HOW IT DOESN'T (2013).
68. Robert G. Kaiser, Op-Ed, *Three Reasons Congress is Broken,* WASH. POST (May 23, 2013), http://articles.washingtonpost.com/2013-05-23/opinions/39470143_1_congress-dodd-frank-bill-culture.
69. TOBIAS A. DORSEY, LEGISLATIVE DRAFTER'S DESKBOOK: A PRACTICAL GUIDE § 2.16 (2006); M. Douglass Bellis, *Drafting in the U.S. Congress,* 22 STATUTE L. REV. 38 (2001) (U.K.). For examples of drafting manuals created by the offices of legislative counsel, see OFFICE OF THE LEGISLATIVE COUNSEL, U.S. SENATE, LEGISLATIVE DRAFTING MANUAL (1997), *available at* http://www.law.yale.edu/documents/pdf/Faculty/SenateOfficeoftheLegislativeCounsel_LegislativeDraftingManual(1997).pdf; OFFICE OF THE LEGISLATIVE COUNSEL, HOUSE LEGISLATIVE COUNSEL'S MANUAL ON DRAFTING STYLE, H.L.C. DOC. NO. 104-1 (1995), *available at* www.house.gov/legcoun/pdf/draftstyle.pdf; BJ Ard, Comment, *Interpreting by the Book: Legislative Drafting Manuals and Statutory Interpretation,* 120 YALE L.J. 185, 187–93 (2010) (describing how the manuals recommend formatting legislation and incorporating canons of construction). In addition, committees may make use of other manuals specific to their individual needs. *See,* e.g., U.S. GEN. ACCOUNTING OFFICE, GAO-04-261SP, PRINCIPLES OF FEDERAL APPROPRIATIONS LAW (3d ed. 2004), *available at* http:/www.gao.gov/special.pubs/d04261sp.pdf (used by appropriations committees). The Supreme Court has from time to time made reference to the drafting manuals in its decisions. *See,* e.g., Carr v. United States, 130 S. Ct. 2229, 2244–46 (2010) (Alito, J., dissenting) (discussing widely accepted legislative drafting conventions); Koons Buick Pontiac GMC, Inc. v. Nigh, 543 U.S. 50, 60–61 (2004) (citing the House and Senate drafting manuals in differentiating between a subparagraph and a clause).

70. Victoria F. Nourse & Jane S. Schacter, *The Politics of Legislative Drafting: A Congressional Case Study*, 77 N.Y.U. L. REV. 575, 588 (2002) (noting that legislative counsel view their involvement as "'strictly up to the client' (i.e., the senator or the committee)").

71. Robert A. Katzmann, *The American Legislative Process as a Signal*, 9 J. PUB. POL'Y 287, 288–89 (1989).

72. Nourse & Schacter, *supra* note 70, at 592–93.

73. *See, e.g.*, Jonathan R. Siegel, *What Statutory Drafting Errors Teach Us About Statutory Interpretation*, 69 GEO. WASH. L. REV. 309, 309, 311–19 (2001) (pointing out an error in the federal venue statute).

74. Nourse & Schacter, *supra* note 70, at 600, 615.

75. *See supra* notes 56–62 and accompanying text.

76. James J. Brudney, *Intentionalism's Revival*, 44 SAN DIEGO L. REV. 1001 (2007).

77. Victoria F. Nourse, *A Decision Theory of Statutory Interpretation: Legislative History by the Rules*, 122 YALE L.J. 70 (2012).

78. Elizabeth Garrett, *The Purposes of Framework Legislation*, 14 J. CONTEMP. LEGAL ISSUES 717 (2005).

79. Abbe R. Gluck & Lisa Schultz Bressman, *Statutory Interpretation From the Inside—An Empirical Study of Congressional Drafting, Delegation and the Canons: Part I*, 65 STAN. L. REV. 901 (2013); Abbe R. Gluck & Lisa Schultz Bressman, *Statutory Interpretation From the Inside—An Empirical Study of Congressional Drafting, Delegation and the Canons: Part II*, 66 STAN. L. REV. 725 (2014).

Chapter 3

1. Peter L. Strauss, *When the Judge Is Not the Primary Official with Responsibility To Read: Agency Interpretation and the Problem of Legislative History*, 66 CHI.-KENT L. REV. 321, 321 (1990). For recent empirical confirmation of Strauss's observations, see Abbe R. Gluck & Lisa Schultz Bressman, *Statutory Interpretation From the Inside—An Empirical Study of Congressional Drafting, Delegation and the Canons: Part II*, 66 STAN. L. REV. 725 (2014). *See also* Jerry L. Mashaw, *Agency-Centered or Court-Centered Administrative Law? A Dialogue with Richard Pierce on Agency Statutory Interpretation*, 59 ADMIN. L. REV. 889, 903 (2007) [hereinafter Mashaw, *Agency-Centered or Court-Centered*] (rejecting the idea that the focus of administrative law should be "even more judicio-centric than it currently is"); Henry P. Monaghan, Marbury *and the Administrative State*, 83 COLUM. L. REV. 1, 25–26 (1983) (noting pre-*Chevron* judicial deference to agency interpretation of law); Trevor W. Morrison, *Constitutional Avoidance in the Executive Branch*, 106 COLUM. L. REV. 1189, 1190 (2006) ("Statutory interpretation is not the exclusive province of the courts; it is a core function of the

executive branch as well."); Edward L. Rubin, *Law and Legislation in the Administrative State*, 89 COLUM. L. REV. 369, 373 (1989) (noting that statutes vest agencies with implementation authority); Cass R. Sunstein & Adrian Vermeule, *Interpretation and Institutions*, 101 MICH. L. REV. 885, 926–27 (2003) (describing Strauss's defense of *Chevron*); Cass R. Sunstein, *Is Tobacco a Drug? Administrative Agencies as Common Law Courts*, 47 DUKE L.J. 1013, 1068 (1998) ("[A]dministrative agencies have become America's common law courts."); Cass R. Sunstein, *Beyond* Marbury: *The Executive's Power To Say What the Law Is*, 115 YALE L.J. 2580, 2583 (2006) (stating that the executive branch is initially responsible for statutory interpretation). *But see* Richard J. Pierce, Jr., *How Agencies Should Give Meaning to the Statutes They Administer: A Response to Mashaw and Strauss*, 59 ADMIN. L. REV. 197, 204 (2007) (disagreeing with Strauss and Mashaw that agencies are "'the primary official interpreters of federal statutes'" (quoting Jerry L. Mashaw, *Norms, Practices, and the Paradox of Deference: A Preliminary Inquiry into Agency Statutory Interpretation*, 57 ADMIN. L. REV. 501, 501–502 (2005) [hereinafter Mashaw, *Norms, Practices, and the Paradox of Deference*]). For more insight into how agencies approach the task of statutory interpretation, see Mashaw, *Norms, Practices, and the Paradox of Deference, supra*, where the author argues for the study of agency statutory interpretation as an autonomous enterprise.

2. HERBERT KAUFMAN, THE ADMINISTRATIVE BEHAVIOR OF FEDERAL BUREAU CHIEFS 47 (1981). *See generally* WALTER J. OLESZEK, CONG. RESEARCH SERV., CONGRESSIONAL OVERSIGHT: AN OVERVIEW (2010), *available at* http://www.fas.org/sgp/crs/misc/R41079.pdf.

3. For more background on how Congress exercises influence over agencies, see generally LAWRENCE C. DODD & RICHARD L. SCHOTT, CONGRESS AND THE ADMINISTRATIVE STATE 155–211 (2d ed. 1986); JOSEPH P. HARRIS, IMPROVING CONGRESSIONAL CONTROL OF ADMINISTRATION (1964); Charles R. Shipan, *Congress and the Bureaucracy, in* THE LEGISLATIVE BRANCH 432, 438–46 (Paul J. Quirk & Sarah A. Binder eds., 2005).

4. For example, John O. Brennan, then CIA director nominee, was asked by Senate Select Intelligence Committee Chair Dianne Feinstein (D-CA):"Do you agree to provide documents or any other materials requested by the Committee in order for it to carry out its oversight and legislative responsibilities?" To which Brennan responded: "Yes; all documents that come under my authority as Director of CIA, I absolutely would." And Senator Feinstein further replied: "We'll talk to you more about that in a minute." *Open Hearing on the Nomination of John O. Brennan To Be Director of the Central Intelligence Agency: Hearings before the S. Select Comm. on Intelligence*, 113th Cong. 27 (2013), *available at* http://www.intelligence.senate.gov/130207/transcript.pdf. For other examples, see ARTHUR MAASS, CONGRESS AND THE COMMON GOOD 183–88 (1983) ("[T]he committees require nominees, as a condition of confirmation,

to make policy-related promises during confirmation hearings."); Steven V. Roberts, *A Lesson in Advising and Consenting*, N.Y. TIMES, Apr. 14, 1983, at B10 (quoting Senator Carl Levin as saying that "[w]e all ask questions at confirmation hearings, hoping to obtain answers that affect future actions").

5. *See generally* JOEL D. ABERBACH, KEEPING A WATCHFUL EYE: THE POLITICS OF CONGRESSIONAL OVERSIGHT (1990) (discussing trends in congressional oversight as well as the politics and processes underlying such oversight); DANIEL CARPENTER, REPUTATION AND POWER 333–34 (2010) (explaining that congressional hearings play a critical role in determining a federal agency's reputation due to the adversarial nature of the hearings and the public testimony presented in them); DANIEL CARPENTER, THE FORGING OF BUREAUCRATIC AUTONOMY: REPUTATIONS, NETWORKS, AND POLICY INNOVATION IN EXECUTIVE AGENCIES, 1862–1928, at 1–3 (2001) (describing an instance in which favorable publicity for a federal agency, generated in part by the agency head, resulted in the transfer of jurisdiction over the forest reserves to the agency even in the face of strong opposition by some members of Congress); CHRISTOPHER H. FOREMAN, JR., SIGNALS FROM THE HILL: CONGRESSIONAL OVERSIGHT AND THE CHALLENGE OF SOCIAL REGULATION 2 (1988) (exploring "the formal tools that Congress employs to oversee administration"); WILLIAM T. GORMLEY, JR. & STEVEN J. BALLA, BUREAUCRACY AND DEMOCRACY: ACCOUNTABILITY AND PERFORMANCE 83 (2d ed. 2007) (noting that oversight as a percentage of total committee activity increased from 9.1 percent in 1971 to 25.2 percent in 1983); DAVID H. ROSENBLOOM, BUILDING A LEGISLATIVE-CENTERED PUBLIC ADMINISTRATION: CONGRESS AND THE ADMINISTRATIVE STATE 1946–1999, at 60–103 (2000) (discussing Congress's role in oversight hearings and general oversight over agencies); Mathew D. McCubbins & Thomas Schwartz, *Congressional Oversight Overlooked: Police Patrols Versus Fire Alarms*, 28 AM. J. POL. SCI. 165 (1984) (arguing that Congress exercises "fire-alarm oversight" over the less effective "police-patrol" oversight); Morris S. Ogul & Bert A. Rockman, *Overseeing Oversight: New Departures and Old Problems*, 15 LEGIS. STUD. Q. 5, 5 (1990) (arguing "that an institutional focus broader than the legislature is essential" for resolving basic problems in legislative oversight).

6. PAUL C. LIGHT, GOVERNMENT BY INVESTIGATION: CONGRESS, PRESIDENT, AND THE SEARCH FOR ANSWERS, 1945–2012 (2013).

7. ROGER H. DAVIDSON, WALTER J. OLESZEK & FRANCES E. LEE, CONGRESS AND ITS MEMBERS 338 (13th ed. 2012).

8. *See* WILLIAM T. GORMLEY, JR., TAMING THE BUREAUCRACY: MUSCLES, PRAYERS, AND OTHER STRATEGIES 159–64 (1989) (describing the effect of GAO reports on agencies).

9. GORMLEY, *supra* note 8.

10. INS v. Chadha, 462 U.S. 919 (1983).

11. Louis Fisher, Cong. Research Serv., Legislative Vetoes After *Chadha* 3–6 (2005); *see also* JESSICA KORN, THE POWER OF SEPARATION: AMERICAN CONSTITUTIONALISM AND THE MYTH OF THE LEGISLATIVE VETO 13 (1996) (arguing that "the legislative veto shortcut was inconsequential to congressional control of the policymaking process").

12. *See*, e.g., James J. Brudney & Corey Ditsler, *The Warp and Woof of Statutory Interpretation: Comparing Supreme Court Approaches in Tax Law and Workplace Law*, 58 DUKE L.J. 1231, 1247, 1270–90 (2009); Michael Livingston, *Congress, the Courts, and the Code: Legislative History and the Interpretation of Tax Statutes*, 69 TEX. L. REV. 819, 832–42 (1991); Bradford L. Ferguson, Frederic W. Hickman & Donald C. Lubick, *Reexamining the Nature and Role of Tax Legislative History in Light of the Changing Realities of the Process*, 67 TAXES 804, 809–12 (1989).

13. *See*, e.g., Chevron U.S.A., Inc. v. Natural Res. Def. Council, Inc., 467 U.S. 837, 843 (1984) ("[I]f the statute is silent or ambiguous with respect to the specific issue, the question for the court is whether the agency's answer is based on a permissible construction of the statute.").

14. *See*, e.g., Mashaw, *Agency-Centered or Court-Centered, supra* note 1; Pierce, *supra* note 1; Strauss, *supra* note 1. Mashaw discusses how such an inquiry might be undertaken. *See* Mashaw, *Norms, Practices, and the Paradox of Deference, supra* note 1, at 524–36 (querying the Federal Register rules database using key search terms as a rudimentary means of identifying agency interpretive methodologies). Pierce rejects the view of Strauss and Mashaw that agencies are primary interpreters of statutes. Pierce, *supra* note 1, at 204. For other thoughtful analsyes, see Catherine M. Sharkey, *Inside Agency Preemption*, 110 MICH. L. REV. 521 (2012); Kevin M. Stack, *Agency Statutory Interpretation and Policymaking Form*, 2009 MICH. ST. L. REV. 225; Kevin M. Stack, *Interpreting Regulations*, 111 MICH. L. REV. 355 (2012).

15. *See generally* WILLIAM D. POPKIN, STATUTES IN COURT: THE HISTORY AND THEORY OF STATUTORY INTERPRETATION 2–3 (1999) (detailing the evolution of statutory interpretation in the United States and recommending the adoption of a "discretionary judicial role" in statutory interpretation); William S. Blatt, *The History of Statutory Interpretation: A Study in Form and Substance*, 6 CARDOZO L. REV. 799 (1985) (chronicling the history of statutory interpretation in the United States and noting the shifting emphasis that courts have placed on form over substance). There are, of course, other theories of statutory construction, apart from those discussed in the succeeding pages, advanced by prominent law professors. *See*, e.g., WILLIAM N. ESKRIDGE, JR., DYNAMIC STATUTORY INTERPRETATION 9 (1994) (endorsing dynamic statutory interpretation, which holds that "the meaning of a statute is not fixed until it is applied to concrete circumstances, and [that] it is neither uncommon nor illegitimate for the meaning of a provision to change over time"); RONALD DWORKIN, LAW'S EMPIRE 313–54

(1986) (advocating an approach to statutory interpretation that accounts for questions of fit, integrity, and political morality).

Chapter 4

1. Judge Henry J. Friendly observed:

> Illogical though it was to hold that a "plain meaning" shut off access to the very materials that might show it not to have been plain at all, it was equally wrong to deny the natural meaning of language its proper primacy; like Cardozo's "Method of Philosophy," it "is the heir presumptive. A pretender to the title will have to fight his way."

Henry J. Friendly, *Mr. Justice Frankfurter and the Reading of Statutes, in* BENCHMARKS 206 (1967) (quoting BENJAMIN N. CARDOZO, THE NATURE OF THE JUDICIAL PROCESS 9, 32 (1921)). *See also* Frederick Schauer, *Statutory Construction and the Coordinating Function of Plain Meaning*, 1990 SUP. CT. REV. 231, 232 ("[T]he reliance on plain meaning serves a stabilizing function...bringing together to some suboptimal equilibrium a process [of coordinating multiple judicial decisionmakers] that might otherwise be much better, but also might otherwise be much worse.").

2. *See,* e.g., Graham County Soil & Water Conservation Dist. v. United States *ex rel.* Wilson, 559 U.S. 280, 303 (2010) (Sotomayor, J., dissenting) ("In my view, the Court misreads the statutory text and gives insufficient weight to contextual and historical evidence of Congress' purpose...."); Barnhart v. Sigmon Coal Co., 534 U.S. 438, 472 (2002) (Stevens, J., dissenting) ("There are occasions when an exclusive focus on text seems to convey an incoherent message....").

3. THE FEDERALIST NO. 37, at 255 (James Madison) (Cynthia Brantley Johnson ed., 2004). It merits a note that Madison and other founders proposed an active role for judges in the legislative process by having members of the Supreme Court serve on a council of revision to help the President exercise the veto power. 2 THE RECORDS OF THE FEDERAL CONVENTION OF 1787, at 73-80 (Max Farrand ed., 1911). Such a scheme, argued Madison, would help "preserv[e] a consistency, conciseness, perspicuity & technical propriety in the laws, qualities peculiarly necessary; & yet shamefully wanting in our republican Codes." FEDERAL CONVENTION OF 1787, at 74. With respect, I think that is one proposal whose rejection was well advised. The pros and cons of the Council proposal are well examined in Russell R. Wheeler, *Extrajudicial Activities of the Early Supreme Court*, 1973 SUP. CT. REV. 123, 127-28 (1973).

4. *See*, e.g., William N. Eskridge, Jr., *All About Words: Early Understandings of the "Judicial Power" in Statutory Interpretation, 1776–1806*, 101 COLUM. L. REV. 990, 990–98 (2001) (providing an historical overview of statutory interpretation at the founding and arguing that judges are agents of as well as partners with Congress, with interpretative authority not confined to the text); John F. Manning, *Deriving Rules of Statutory Interpretation from the Constitution*, 101 COLUM. L. REV. 1648, 1648–53 (2001) (contending that although the founders did not definitively resolve the judiciary's relationship with Congress, they developed a constitutional structure that fits better with the faithful agent theory and textualism than the coequal partner model).

5. *See* Philip A. Hamburger, *Natural Rights, Natural Law, and American Constitutions*, 102 YALE L.J. 907, 954 (1993) ("[F]ar from being a practicable measure for determining which laws accorded with a constitution and which did not, natural law tended to be a theoretical explanation of limitations on natural rights.").

6. *See* Adrian Vermeule, *The Cycles of Statutory Interpretation*, 68 U. CHI. L. REV. 149 (2001) (arguing that courts have changed their interpretative practices with some frequency).

7. As Justice Breyer stated: "Only by seeking that purpose can we avoid the substitution of judicial for legislative will. Only by reading language in its light can we maintain the democratic link between voters, legislators, statutes, and ultimate implementation, upon which the legitimacy of our constitutional system rests." Arlington Cent. Sch. Dist. Bd. of Educ. v. Murphy, 548 U.S. 291, 323–24 (2006) (Breyer, J., dissenting). Justice Breyer has written that he finds "purposes and consequences…most helpful most often…to help unlock the meaning of a statutory text." STEPHEN BREYER, MAKING OUR DEMOCRACY WORK: A JUDGE'S VIEW 88 (2010). As to consequences, he writes: "The judge also examines the likely consequences of a proposed interpretation, asking whether they are more likely to further than to hinder achievement of the provision's purpose." BREYER, MAKING OUR DEMOCRACY WORK, at 92.

8. Heydon's Case, (1584) 76 Eng. Rep. 637 (K.B.) 638; 3 Co. Rep. 7a, 7b.

9. Church of the Holy Trinity v. United States, 143 U.S. 457 (1892).

10. Alien Contract Labor Act of 1885, ch. 164, § 1, 23 Stat. 332, 332 (amended 1888).

11. *Holy Trinity*, 143 U.S. at 459.

12. *Holy Trinity*, 143 U.S. at 463 (quoting United States v. Craig, 28 F. 795, 798 (C.C.E.D. Mich. 1886)).

13. *Holy Trinity*, 143 U.S. at 464–65.

14. *Holy Trinity*, 143 U.S. at 471.

15. *See* William S. Blatt, *Missing the Mark: An Overlooked Statute Redefines the Debate over Statutory Interpretation*, 104 NW. U. L. REV. COLLOQUY 147, 150 (2009), available at http://www.law.northwestern.edu/lawreview/colloquy/2009/36/ ("Long after it was decided, *Holy Trinity* was regarded as an important case,

both for its willingness to depart from text, and for its reliance on legislative history."). Professor Eskridge, and later Professor Blatt, have noted that pre–*Holy Trinity*, the 1891 edition of Sutherland's *Statutes and Statutory Construction* did not make specific reference to use of committee reports; however, the 1904 edition stated that committee reports were "proper sources of information in ascertaining the intent or meaning of an act." Blatt, *Missing the Mark*, at 150 n. 23 (quoting 2 J.G. SUTHERLAND, STATUTES AND STATUTORY CONSTRUCTION § 470, at 879–80 (John Lewis ed., 2d ed. 1904) (citing *Holy Trinity*)). *See* WILLIAM N. ESKRIDGE, JR., DYNAMIC STATUTORY INTERPRETATION 208–09 (1994); *see also* Carol Chomsky, *Unlocking the Mysteries of* Holy Trinity: *Spirit, Letter, and History in Statutory Interpretation*, 100 COLUM. L. REV. 901, 907 (2000) ("*Holy Trinity Church* establishes the importance of recourse to legislative history and affords a...foundation for non-textualist approaches to statutory interpretation...."); Bradley C. Karkkainen, *"Plain Meaning": Justice Scalia's Jurisprudence of Strict Statutory Construction*, 17 HARV. J.L. & PUB. POL'Y 401, 434 n.132 (1994) ("The earliest Supreme Court case commonly cited for the use of legislative history to construe a statute is Church of the Holy Trinity v. United States."); Lawrence M. Solan, *Law, Language, and Lenity*, 40 WM. & MARY L. REV. 57, 97 (1998) (noting that "*Holy Trinity* presaged a gradual change in the Supreme Court's methodology" toward greater reliance on legislative history in statutory interpretation). For a critique of the use of legislative history in *Holy Trinity*, see Adrian Vermeule, *Legislative History and the Limits of Judicial Competence: The Untold Story of* Holy Trinity Church, 50 STAN. L. REV. 1833, 1836 (1998), where the author uses *Holy Trinity* as the starting point to argue that the structural constraints of governing the adjudicatory process undermine the judiciary's ability to accurately discern legislative intent from legislative history.

16. *See, e.g.*, William N. Eskridge, Jr., *"Fetch Some Soupmeat,"* 16 CARDOZO L. REV. 2209, 2217 n.38 (1995) ("*Church of the Holy Trinity* has...been the focal point of the debate between the Supreme Court's 'new textualists' and more purpose-based interpreters."); Frederick Schauer, *Constitutional Invocations*, 65 FORDHAM L. REV. 1295, 1307 (1997) ("*Church of the Holy Trinity v. United States* is not only a case, but is the marker for an entire legal tradition,...[one which emphasizes that] there is far more to law than the plain meaning of authoritative legal texts...."). Nicholas Parrillo reports that it was not until the 1940s when judicial use of legislative history became routine, reflecting, he argues, the newly-expanded New Deal administrative state. Nicholas R. Parrillo, *Leviathan and Interpretive Revolution: The Administrative State, the Judiciary, and the Rise of Legislative History, 1890–1950*, 123 YALE L.J. 266 (2013).

17. *See* Antonin Scalia, *Common-Law Courts in a Civil-Law System: The Role of United States Federal Courts in Interpreting the Constitution and Laws*, in A MATTER OF INTERPRETATION: FEDERAL COURTS AND THE FEDERAL LAW 3,

22 (Amy Gutmann ed., 1997) (criticizing *Holy Trinity* and its inquiry beyond the text into legislative intent). Justice Scalia's view echoes the approach taken by Judge William J. Wallace, the lower court judge whose decision the Supreme Court reversed in *Holy Trinity*. While acknowledging the likely purpose of the statute is in conflict with a literal reading of the text, Judge Wallace nevertheless held:

> [W]here the terms of a statute are plain, unambiguous, and explicit, the courts are not at liberty to go outside of the language to search for a meaning which it does not reasonably bear in the effort to ascertain and give effect to what may be imagined to have been or not to have been the intention of congress. Whenever the will of congress is declared in ample and unequivocal language, that will must be absolutely followed, and it is not admissible to resort to speculations of policy, nor even to the views of members of congress in debate, to find reasons to control or modify the statute.

United States v. Church of the Holy Trinity, 36 F. 303, 304 (C.C.S.D.N.Y. 1888).

18. Learned Hand, *How Far Is a Judge Free in Rendering a Decision?*, *in* Nat'l Advisory Council on Radio in Educ., Law Series I 1 (1935), *reprinted in* The Spirit of Liberty 103, 106 (Irving Dilliard ed., 1952).

19. *See* Henry M. Hart, Jr. & Albert M. Sacks, The Legal Process: Basic Problems in the Making and Application of Law (William N. Eskridge, Jr. & Philip P. Frickey eds., 1994) [hereinafter Hart & Sacks]. Hart and Sacks's materials had, until 1994—when they were formally published through the efforts of William N. Eskridge, Jr. and Philip P. Frickey—been disseminated as "a '[t]entative [e]dition.'" Erwin N. Griswold, *Preface* to Hart & Sacks, *supra*, at vii, vii–ix (describing the decades-long effort to publish Hart and Sacks's work). The 1994 publication consists of the 1958 tentative edition. William N. Eskridge, Jr. & Philip P. Frickey, *Publication Editors' Preface* to Hart & Sacks, *supra*, at xi. Norman Dorsen, the Madison Lecture's impresario, developed extensive supplemental materials to the Hart and Sacks work.

20. Hart & Sacks, *supra* note 19, at 1374.

21. Hart & Sacks, supra note 19, at 1376. For a discussion of the legal process school, see Robert Post, *Theorizing Disagreement: Reconceiving the Relationship Between Law and Politics*, 98 Calif. L. Rev. 1319, 1332–36 (2010).

22. *See* Breyer, *supra* note 7, at 88 (linking "whether [the Court's] interpretations will effectively carry out the statute's objectives" to "whether its relationship with Congress will tend more toward the cooperative or the confrontational"); Linda Greenhouse, *Making Congress All It Can Be*, N.Y. Times Opinionator Blog (Oct. 7, 2010, 9:38 p.m.), http://opinionator.blogs.nytimes.com/2010/10/07/making-congress-all-it-can-be/?action=click&module=Search&region=search

Results%230&version=&url=http%3A%2F%2Fquery.nytimes.com%2Fsearch
%2Fsitesearch%2F%3Faction%3Dclick%26region%3DMasthead%26pgtype%
3DHomepage%26module%3DSearchSubmit%26contentCollection%3DHom
epage%26t%3Dqry920%23%2Flinda%2520greenhouse%2520making%2520c
ongress%2520work%2520opinionator%2520blog (noting that Justice Breyer
views the Supreme Court as helping Congress). Justice Breyer has long advo-
cated the use of legislative history as a tool for statutory interpretation. *See*
Stephen Breyer, *On the Uses of Legislative History in Interpreting Statutes*, 65 S.
CAL. L. REV. 845 (1992). *See generally* ROBERT A. KATZMANN, COURTS AND
CONGRESS (1997) (advancing the view that courts and Congress should work
together) [hereinafter KATZMANN, COURTS AND CONGRESS]; JUDGES AND
LEGISLATORS: TOWARD INSTITUTIONAL COMITY (Robert A. Katzmann ed.,
1988) (same). Jeffrey Rosen notes that historically some chief justices con-
sciously viewed the Court as a partner of Congress rather than as an adversary.
Jeffrey Rosen, *Can the Judicial Branch be a Steward in a Polarized Society?*,
DÆDALUS, Spring 2013, at 28.

23. Kenneth A. Shepsle, *Congress is a "They," Not an "It": Legislative Intent as Oxymoron*,
12 INT'L REV. L. & ECON. 239, 239 (1992).

24. *See* A. Raymond Randolph, *Dictionaries, Plain Meaning, and Context in Statutory
Interpretation*, 17 HARV. J.L. & PUB. POL'Y 71, 77 (1994) (explaining how analysis of legislative history supplements rigorous textual analysis by enabling a
judge to "test[] his tentative construction of the statutory language"). For an
example of how legislative history has been used to construe the meaning of a
specialized term in the context of a complex statutory scheme, see Solite Corp.
v. EPA, 952 F.2d 473, 492–93 (D.C. Cir. 1991), where the court analyzed
whether the Bevill Amendment to Subtitle C of the Resource Conservation and
Recovery Act applies to various waste categories, including lightweight aggre-
gate air pollution dust, lead process wastewater, or chrome tailings.

25. Barnhart v. Sigmon Coal Co., 534 U.S. 438, 472 (2002) (Stevens, J., dissenting).

26. See, for example, Justice Sotomayor's opinion in *Carr v. United States*, 130 S. Ct.
2229, 2241–42 (2010), where the Court used legislative history to supplement
textual analysis in determining whether a provision of the Sex Offender
Registration and Notification Act that criminalized interstate travel of unregis-
tered sex offenders was intended to apply to sex offenders who traveled before
the passage of the Act, and Justice Kagan's opinion in *Tapia v. United States*, 131
S. Ct. 2382, 2391 (2011), where the Court observed that the legislative history
provided further confirmation of the use of textual analysis in determining
whether the Sentencing Reform Act precludes federal courts from lengthening
a prison term to promote rehabilitation.

27. *Interbranch Relations: Hearings Before the Joint Comm. on the Org. of Cong.*, 103d Cong.
77, 277 (1993) (statement of Robert W. Kastenmeier, Fellow, Governance Inst.).

28. *Nomination of Judge Antonin Scalia: Hearings Before the S. Comm. on the Judiciary
on the Nomination of Antonin Scalia, To Be Associate Justice of the Supreme Court*

of the United States, 99th Cong. 65–66 (1986) (statement of Sen. Charles E. Grassley).

29. *Confirmation Hearing on the Nomination of John G. Roberts, Jr. To Be Chief Justice of the United States: Hearing Before the S. Comm. on the Judiciary*, 109th Cong. 318–19 (2005) (statement of Sen. Charles E. Grassley). A few months later, Senator Grassley would question then-Judge Samuel A. Alito, Jr., on his views of legislative history. *See Confirmation Hearing on the Nomination of Judge Samuel A. Alito, Jr. To Be an Associate Justice of the Supreme Court of the United States: Hearing Before the S. Comm. on the Judiciary*, 109th Cong. 503 (2006) (statement of Sen. Charles E. Grassley).

30. Orrin Hatch, *Legislative History: Tool of Construction or Destruction*, 11 HARV. J.L. & PUB. POL'Y 43, 43 (1988).

31. Hatch, *supra* note 30, at 47.

32. Joan Biskupic, *Scalia Takes a Narrow View in Seeking Congress' Will*, 48 CONG. Q. WKLY. REP. 913, 917 (1990) (alteration in original). At the most recent Supreme Court confirmation hearing, that of Elena Kagan, Senator Al Franken (D-MN), criticized a Supreme Court decision for not looking into legislative history, and urged the nominee to consider such history, observing that "we spend a lot of time in hearings and on the floor debating legislation." *The Nomination of Elena Kagan To Be an Associate Justice of the United States: Hearing Before the S. Comm. on the Judiciary*, 111th Cong. 219 (2010) (statement of Sen. Al Franken).

33. Abbe R. Gluck & Lisa Schultz Bressman, *Statutory Interpretation From the Inside—An Empirical Study of Congressional Drafting, Delegation and the Canons: Part I*, 65 STAN. L. REV. 901, 965 (2013).

34. Gluck & Bressman, *supra* note 33, at 964–89.

35. Arlington Cent. Sch. Dist. Bd. of Educ. v. Murphy, 548 U.S. 291, 324 (2006) (Breyer, J., dissenting).

36. Conroy v. Aniskoff, 507 U.S. 511, 519 (1993) (Scalia, J., concurring) (emphasis omitted) (quoting Aldridge v. Williams, 44 U.S. (3 How.) 9, 24 (1845)).

37. INS v. Cardoza-Fonseca, 480 U.S. 421, 453 (1987) (Scalia, J., concurring).

38. Wis. Pub. Intervenor v. Mortier, 501 U.S. 597, 620 (1991) (Scalia, J., concurring in the judgment).

39. Blanchard v. Bergeron, 489 U.S. 87, 98–99 (1989) (Scalia, J., concurring in part and concurring in the judgment).

40. Thompson v. Thompson, 484 U.S. 174, 192 (1988) (Scalia, J., concurring) (citation omitted).

41. As then–D.C. Circuit Judge Scalia wrote: "[R]outine deference to the detail of committee reports ... [is] converting a system of judicial construction into a system of committee-staff prescription." Hirschey v. Fed. Energy Regulatory Comm'n, 777 F.2d 1, 8 (D.C. Cir. 1985) (Scalia, J., concurring).

42. *See* John F. Manning, *Textualism as a Nondelegation Doctrine*, 97 COLUM. L. REV. 673, 698 (1997) ("[T]extualists have opened a second front in pressing their

constitutional objections to the authority of legislative history—Lockean non-delegation principles.") [hereinafter Manning, *Textualism*].

43. Scalia, *supra* note 17, at 36 ("In any major piece of legislation, the legislative history is extensive, and there is something for everybody.... The variety and specificity of result that legislative history can achieve is unparalleled.").

44. *See generally* JAMES M. BUCHANAN & GORDON TULLOCK, THE CALCULUS OF CONSENT: LOGICAL FOUNDATIONS OF CONSTITUTIONAL DEMOCRACY (1962) (outlining principles of public choice theory); DANIEL A. FARBER & PHILIP P. FRICKEY, LAW AND PUBLIC CHOICE: A CRITICAL INTRODUCTION 21–33 (1991) (same); William C. Mitchell & Michael C. Munger, *Economic Models of Interest Groups: An Introductory Survey*, 35 AM. J. POL. SCI. 512 (1991) (reviewing several scholars' earlier models of how interest groups influence policies); Susan Rose-Ackerman, Comment, *Progressive Law and Economics—and the New Administrative Law*, 98 YALE L.J. 341, 344–47 (1988) (outlining public choice theory).

45. *See, e.g.*, Frank H. Easterbrook, *The Supreme Court, 1983 Term—Foreword: The Court and the Economic System*, 98 HARV. L. REV. 4, 45–51 (1984) (observing that the Supreme Court has, through its opinions, become more sympathetic to the public choice/interest group approach toward legislation); Richard A. Epstein, *Toward a Revitalization of the Contract Clause*, 51 U. CHI. L. REV. 703, 704 (1984) (noting that an interest group's ability to influence legislation has been used as a justification for very limited constitutional protection of economic liberties); Jonathan R. Macey, *Promoting Public-Regarding Legislation Through Statutory Interpretation: An Interest Group Model*, 86 COLUM. L. REV. 223, 226 (1986) (arguing that the judiciary, through its interpretation of statutes, serves as a critical check on the ability of private interest groups to advance their particular interests at the expense of the public); Geoffrey P. Miller, *Public Choice at the Dawn of the Special Interest State: The Story of Butter and Margarine*, 77 CALIF. L. REV. 83 (1989) (applying public choice principles to examine the history of the American dairy industry's efforts to pass laws discriminating against margarine).

46. *See, e.g.*, Peter H. Aronson, Ernest Gellhorn & Glen O. Robinson, *A Theory of Legislation Delegation*, 68 CORNELL L. REV. 1, 37–62 (1982) (describing responsibility-shifting and lottery models). *But see* Jerry L. Mashaw, *Prodelegation: Why Administrators Should Make Political Decisions*, 1 J.L. ECON. & ORG. 81, 85–91 (1985) (critiquing opponents of the delegation doctrine).

47. MANCUR OLSON, THE LOGIC OF COLLECTIVE ACTION: PUBLIC GOODS AND THE THEORY OF GROUPS 2 (1971) (emphasis omitted).

48. *See, e.g.*, MORRIS P. FIORINA, CONGRESS: KEYSTONE OF THE WASHINGTON ESTABLISHMENT 39–49 (1977) (describing a self-interested congressional establishment concerned primarily with its own reelection).

49. Blanchard v. Bergeron, 489 U.S. 87, 98–99 (1989) (Scalia, J., concurring in part and concurring in the judgment).

50. John F. Manning, *Second Generation Textualism*, 98 CALIF. L. REV. 1287, 1309–10 (2010) (emphasis added).

51. *See* Adam Liptak, *Justices Turning More Frequently to Dictionary, and Not Just for Big Words*, N.Y. TIMES, June 14, 2011, at A11 (noting that Supreme Court Justices have increased their use and citation of dictionaries to aid in interpreting statutory language).

52. In earlier writings, Professor Manning did leave open a narrow window for the use of legislative history when it supplies "an objective, unmanufactured history of a statute's context." Manning, *Textualism, supra* note 42, at 731. He wrote:

> If such legislative history *persuasively* describes that objective context (rather than merely offering the committee's or sponsor's own idiosyncratic expression of intent), a court may consider that history for "'the thoroughness evident in its consideration, the validity of its reasoning, its consistency with earlier and later pronouncements, and all those facters [sic] which give it power to persuade, if lacking power to control.'"

John F. Manning, *Putting Legislative History to a Vote: A Response to Professor Siegel*, 53 VAND. L. REV. 1529, 1529 n.2 (2000) (quoting Manning, *Textualism, supra* note 42, at 733 n.252 (quoting Skidmore v. Swift & Co., 323 U.S. 134, 140 (1944))).

53. Abbe R. Gluck & Lisa Schultz Bressman, *Statutory Interpretation from the Inside—An Empirical Study of Congressional Drafting, Delegation and the Canons: Part I*, 65 STAN. L. REV. 901, 938 (2013).

54. *See* James J. Brudney & Lawrence Baum, *Oasis or Mirage: The Supreme Court's Thirst for Dictionaries in the Rehnquist and Roberts Eras*, 55 WM. & MARY L. REV. 483 (2013).

55. Brudney & Baum, *supra* note 54.

56. *See, e.g.,* FARBER & FRICKEY, *supra* note 44, at 116–17 (discussing the limitations of public choice theory); KATZMANN, COURTS AND CONGRESS, *supra* note 22, at 52–53 (criticizing the public choice view as oversimplified and noting that Congress sometimes acts without interest group support or despite powerful opposition); THE POLITICS OF REGULATION (James Q. Wilson ed., 1980); Robert A. Katzmann, *Comments on Levine and Forrence, "Regulatory Capture, Public Interest, and the Public Agenda: Toward a Synthesis,"* 6 J.L. ECON. & ORG. 199 (1990) (discussing several possible reasons for legislative and regulatory outcomes outside of the paradigmatic public choice analysis).

57. On agenda setting, see BRIAN D. JONES & FRANK R. BAUMGARTNER, THE POLITICS OF ATTENTION (2005), where the authors examine how policymakers obtain and use information to set the agenda, and JOHN W. KINGDON, AGENDAS, ALTERNATIVES, AND PUBLIC POLICIES (2d ed. 2011), where the author explores how issues become part of the public agenda.

58. R. Shep Melnick found little interest group involvement in his studies of the food stamp program, aid to families with dependent children, and special education. *See* R. SHEP MELNICK, BETWEEN THE LINES: INTERPRETING WELFARE RIGHTS 259–60 (1994) (noting that legislators' desires to advance what they believed to be good public policy were driving forces in the development of these policies as well as broader public opinion).

59. *See* James Q. Wilson, *The Politics of Regulation, in* THE POLITICS OF REGULATION, *supra* note 56, at 357, 357–72 (assessing non-economic reasons driving the politics of regulation).

60. *See* ROBERT A. KATZMANN, INSTITUTIONAL DISABILITY: THE SAGA OF TRANSPORTATION POLICY FOR THE DISABLED 189 n.1 (1986) (arguing that in the case of the disability rights movement, "policy origination owe[d] little to 'interest group liberalism'").

61. *See* MARTHA DERTHICK & PAUL J. QUIRK, THE POLITICS OF DEREGULATION 16–19 (1985) (noting that industry interests were vehemently opposed to the deregulation of the air transport, trucking, and wireline telephone industries); Wilson, *supra* note 59, at 357–72 (reviewing various regulatory proposals and analyzing their sources of political support).

62. DAVID R. MAYHEW, CONGRESS: THE ELECTORAL CONNECTION 13 (1974).

63. *See, e.g.,* MELNICK, *supra* note 58, at 260 (noting that legislators' desires to advance what they believed to be good public policy were driving forces in the development of these policies as well as broader public opinion).

64. Martin D. Ginsburg, Luncheon Speech at the New York State Bar Association Tax Section Annual Meeting Luncheon (Jan. 24, 1991), *reprinted in Interbranch Relations, supra* note 27, at 293–95 (noting that in the area of tax legislation, many provisions in the committee reports are not read by members of Congress).

65. Observing that he was "considerably involved in writing" the "uniform capitalization rules" in a contemporary tax bill, Senator Moynihan contended that these rules—designed to provide a better matching of income and expenses of manufacturing property—did not apply to books. Daniel Patrick Moynihan, Letter to the Editor, *How To Tell a Manufacturer from a Writer*, N.Y. TIMES, Sept. 6, 1987, at E14. However, a footnote in a conference committee report that later became law did appear to encompass books. Senator Moynihan was moved to write:

> I was a member of the conference committee. I do not ever recall the subject's having been raised, nor does any senator or representative with whom I've talked. My best guess is that staff members wrote it into the report thinking it was *already* law.... It is not law, and must not be construed as law.

Moynihan, *Letter to the Times.*

66. Joan Biskupic, *Congress Keeps Eye on Justices as Court Watches Hill's Words*, 49 CONG. Q. WKLY. REP. 2863, 2863 (1991).

67. Biskupic, *supra* note 66.

68. When Justice Scalia rebuked Justice Alito's use of legislative history in *Zedner v. United States*, 547 U.S. 489, 509–11 (Scalia, J., concurring in part and concurring in the judgment), the mainstream media took notice. *See* Tony Mauro, *Alito the Latest To Feel Scalia's Sting*, LEGAL TIMES, June 6, 2006, at 8. *See also* JEFFREY TOOBIN, THE NINE: INSIDE THE WORLD OF THE SUPREME COURT 369 (2007).

69. Hughes Aircraft Co. v. Jacobson, 525 U.S. 432, 438 (1999); *see also* United States v. Gayle, 342 F.3d 89, 92 (2d Cir. 2003) ("Statutory construction begins with the plain text and, if that text is unambiguous, it usually ends there as well.").

70. Citizens to Preserve Overton Park v. Volpe, 401 U.S. 402, 412 n.29 (1971).

71. Exxon Mobil Corp. v. Allapattah Servs., Inc., 545 U.S. 546, 568 (2005) (quoting Patricia M. Wald, *Some Observations on the Use of Legislative History in the 1981 Supreme Court Term*, 68 IOWA L. REV. 195, 214 (1983)).

72. *See, e.g.,* William N. Eskridge, Jr. & Lauren E. Baer, *The Continuum of Deference: Supreme Court Treatment of Agency Statutory Interpretation from* Chevron *to* Hamdan, 97 GEO. L.J. 1083, 1135–36 (2008) (noting that the Supreme Court uses legislative history in the *Chevron* inquiry).

73. *See generally* FRANK B. CROSS, THE THEORY AND PRACTICE OF STATUTORY INTERPRETATION 59 (2009) (noting that even proponents of legislative history acknowledge that its use must be grounded first in the text, for they "do not disregard the text, they seek to illuminate it"); James J. Brudney, *Confirmatory Legislative History*, 76 BROOK. L. REV. 901 (2011) (discussing the use of legislative history as a tool for judges to confirm and complete conclusions they have already reached) [hereinafter Brudney, *Confirmatory*]; James J. Brudney & Corey Ditslear, *The Decline and Fall of Legislative History? Patterns of Supreme Court Reliance in the Berger and Rehnquist Eras*, 89 JUDICATURE 220 (2006) (noting the sharp decline in the Court's interest in legislative history over time); James J. Brudney & Corey Ditslear, *The Warp and Woof of Statutory Interpretation: Comparing Supreme Court Approaches in Tax Law and Workplace Law*, 58 DUKE L.J. 1231 (2009) (identifying an overall decline in the use of legislative history, but pointing out that the Court continues to use legislative history to identify congressional bargains or to borrow expertise from a more knowledgeable branch, depending on the substantive area of law); Michael H. Koby, *The Supreme Court's Declining Reliance on Legislative History: The Impact of Justice Scalia's Critique*, 36 HARV. J. ON LEGIS. 369, 369 (1999) (positing that Justice Scalia has "contributed significantly to a sharp reduction in the Court's use of legislative history"); David S. Law & David Zaring, *Law Versus Ideology: The Supreme Court and the Use of Legislative History*, 51 WM. & MARY L. REV. 1653 (2010) (discussing the use of legislative history); Glenn Bridgman, *One of These Things Is Not Like the Others: Legislative History in the U.S. Courts of Appeal* (Yale

Law Sch. Student Prize Papers, No. 88, 2012), *available at* http://digitalcom-mons.law.yale.edu/ylsspps_papers/88/(examining uses of legislative history in Courts of Appeals).

74. Mohamad v. Palestinian Auth., 132 S. Ct. 1702, 1710 (2012).

75. Tapia v. United States, 131 S. Ct. 2382, 2388, 2390, 2391 (2011).

76. *Nomination of Ruth Bader Ginsburg, To Be Associate Justice of the Supreme Court of the United States: Hearings Before the S. Comm. on the Judiciary*, 103d Cong. 224 (1993).

77. *See* Elena Kagan, *Presidential Administration*, 114 HARV. L. REV. 2245, 2255 (2001) (discussing the inability or unwillingness of Congress to legislate specific solutions to problems and noting its preference for general delegations of power); Edward L. Rubin, *Law and Legislation in the Administrative State*, 89 COLUM. L. REV. 369, 411 (1989) (expressing a preference for goal-oriented statutes that leave the precise implementation to agencies, given the complexity of the issues that face Congress). On the politics of delegation, see generally JAMES H. COX, REVIEWING DELEGATION: AN ANALYSIS OF THE CONGRESSIONAL REAUTHORIZATION PROCESS (2004), and DAVID EPSTEIN & SHARYN O'HALLORAN, DELEGATING POWERS (1999). For the view that Congress some-times crafts legislation recognizing that courts will ultimately have to resolve open questions, see GEORGE I. LOVELL, LEGISLATIVE DEFERRALS: STATUTORY AMBIGUITY, JUDICIAL POWER, AND AMERICAN DEMOCRACY 253 (2003).

78. Richard B. Stewart, *Beyond Delegation Doctrine*, 36 AM. U. L. REV. 323, 331 (1987).

79. *See* Daniel J. Meltzer, *The Supreme Court's Judicial Passivity*, 2002 SUP. CT. REV. 343, 387 ("An absence of textual specification may equally reflect the incapacity of legis-lators, no matter how willing to try to resolve statutory uncertainties, to anticipate all of the uncertainties that will arise, as well as the difficulties of crafting language that, in the myriad contexts to which it is applied, will avoid ambiguity.").

80. HERBERT KAUFMAN, TIME, CHANCE AND ORGANIZATIONS: NATURAL SELECTION IN A PERILOUS ENVIRONMENT 52 (1985); *see also* Stephen B. Burbank, *Procedure, Politics and Power: The Role of Congress*, 79 NOTRE DAME L. REV. 1677, 1681 (2004) ("Another reason may be the incentive of any institu-tion (and of those who champion that institution) to prefer ambiguity when clarity might diminish its power or prestige.") (citing Joseph A. Grundfest & A.C. Pritchard, *Statutes with Multiple Personality Disorders: The Value of Ambiguity in Statutory Design and Interpretation*, 54 STAN. L. REV. 627 (2002) (explaining the role of ambiguity in reaching compromise in Congress)).

81. *See* Elizabeth Garrett, *Legal Scholarship in the Age of Legislation*, 34 TULSA L.J. 679, 688 (1999) (calling for more empirical scholarship on how Congress func-tions to test theories such as textualism).

82. *See, e.g.*, James H. Hutson, *The Creation of the Constitution: The Integrity of the Documentary Record*, 65 TEX. L. REV. 1 (1986).

83. James J. Brudney, *Intentionalism's Revival*, 44 SAN DIEGO L. REV. 1001, 1009–10 (2007); Jonathan R. Siegel, *The Use of Legislative History in a System of Separated Powers*, 53 VAND. L. REV. 1457, 1480 (2000). *But see* Manning, *Textualism, supra* note 42, at 706–25 (arguing that interpretative reliance on legislative history creates an opportunity for legislative self-delegation, contrary to the clear assumption of constitutional structure).

84. *See supra* Chapter Two, note 69 and accompanying text (noting established drafting rules and practices in the Senate and House). For an interesting view suggesting that Congress could legislate doctrines of statutory construction, see Nicholas Quinn Rosenkranz, *Federal Rules of Statutory Interpretation*, 115 HARV. L. REV. 2085 (2002).

85. Brudney, *Confirmatory, supra* note 73, at 1010.

86. James J. Brudney, *Congressional Commentary on Judicial Interpretations of Statues: Idle Chatter or Telling Response?*, 93 MICH. L. REV. 1, 49–50 (1994).

87. Victoria F. Nourse, *A Decision Theory of Statutory Interpretation: Legislative History by the Rules*, 122 YALE L.J. 70 (2012).

88. Nourse, *supra* note 87, at 78.

89. Gluck & Bressman, *supra* note 53.

90. ANTONIN SCALIA & BRYAN A. GARNER, READING LAW: THE INTERPRETATION OF LEGAL TEXTS (2012).

91. SCALIA & GARNER, *supra* note 90, at 56.

92. SCALIA & GARNER, *supra* note 90, at 234.

93. SCALIA & GARNER, *supra* note 90, at 247–51.

94. SCALIA & GARNER, *supra* note 90, at 290–94

95. SCALIA & GARNER, *supra* note 90, at 296–302.

96. SCALIA & GARNER, *supra* note 90, at 369–91.

97. Karl N. Llewllyn, *Remarks on the Theory of Appellate Decision and the Rules or Canons About How Statues are to Be Construed*, 3 VAND. L. REV. 395 (1950); KARL N. LLEWLLYN, THE COMMON LAW TRADITION: DECIDING APPEALS (1960).

98. *See, e.g.,* SCALIA & GARNER, *supra* note 90, at 59–60.

99. See Raila v. United States, 355 F.3d 118 (2d Cir. 2004), and United States ex rel. Kirk v. Schindler Elevator Corp., 601 F.3d 94 (2d Cir. 2010). *Raila* is discussed in Chapter 5.

100. RICHARD A. POSNER, THE FEDERAL COURTS: CRISIS AND REFORM 276 (1985). For a recent Posner critique, see RICHARD A. POSNER, REFLECTIONS ON JUDGING 199–219 (2013).

101. SCALIA & GARNER, *supra* note 90, at 59.

102. *See* William N. Eskridge, Jr., *The New Textualism and Normative Canons*, 113 COLUM. L. REV. 531, 544 (2013). J. Willard Hurst long ago recognized that the existence of dueling canons without a key may actually enlarge judicial discretion rather than confine it. J. WILLARD HURST, DEALING WITH STATUTES 65 (1982).

103. Abner J. Mikva, *Reading and Writing Statutes*, 48 U. Pitt. L. Rev. 627, 629 (1987).
104. Gluck & Bressman, *supra* note 53, at 932–33.
105. Gluck & Bressman, *supra* note 53, at 907.
106. For a thoughtful discussion, see Cass R. Sunstein, *Interpreting Statutes in the Regulatory State*, 103 Harv. L. Rev. 405 (1989); William N. Eskridge, Jr., *Public Values in Statutory Interpretation*, 137 U. Pa. L. Rev. 1007 (1989).
107. *Statutory Interpretation and the Uses of Legislative History: Hearing Before Subcomm. on Courts, Intellectual Property, and the Administration of Justice of the H. Comm. on the Judiciary*, 101st Cong. 52 (1990) (statement of Stephen G. Breyer).
108. *Confirmation Hearing on the Nomination of John G. Roberts, Jr. To Be Chief Justice of the United States: Hearing Before the S. Comm. on the Judiciary*, 109th Cong. 319 (2005) (statement of Sen. Charles E. Grassley).
109. Hatch, *supra* note 30, at 43.
110. Nourse, *supra* note 87, at 76 (arguing for "a rule of reverse sequential consideration: legislative history should focus on the last relevant legislative decision").

Chapter 5

1. For a thoughtful discussion recognizing the legitimacy of multiple approaches and factors, see Todd D. Rakoff, *Statutory Interpretation as a Multifarious Enterprise*, 104 Nw. U. L. Rev. 1559, 1569–86 (2010).
2. Commenting on the challenge of developing a "grand theory" of judicial decision-making, Judge Frank Coffin wrote: "I suspect that any such attempt is about as likely to succeed as trying to shoehorn an elephant's foot into a ballet slipper." Frank M. Coffin, U.S. Senior Circuit Judge, My Judicial Key Ring: Remarks upon Receipt of the Morton A. Brody 2006 Award for Distinguished Judicial Service at Colby College 4 (Mar. 19, 2006) (transcript on file with author).
3. Benjamin Franklin, A Proposal To Promote Useful Knowledge Among the British Plantations in America 1 (1743), *available at* http://nationalhumanitiescenter.org/pds/becomingamer/ideas/text4/amerphilsociety.pdf.
4. *See, e.g.*, Henry J. Friendly, *Mr. Justice Frankfurter and the Reading of Statutes*, *in* Benchmarks 206 (1967) (emphasizing that statutes come in varying levels of specificity and open-endedness); Pierre N. Leval, *Trademark: Champion of Free Speech*, 27 Colum. J.L. & Arts 187, 195–98 (2004) (dividing statutes into "micromanager" statutes and "delegating" statutes that either adopt the common law or make "new policy").
5. Lexecon, Inc. v. Milberg Weiss Bershad Hynes & Lerach, 523 U.S. 26, 37 (1998).
6. 21 U.S.C. § 844(a) (2006).
7. *See* United States v. Morgan, 412 F. App'x 357, 359–60 (2d Cir. 2011) (rejecting the appellant's claim that his purchase of pseudoephedrine for personal

consumption did not violate the statute because Congress's purpose, on his argument, was to prevent the manufacture of methamphetamine).

8. 18 U.S.C. §1519 (2006) (emphasis added).

9. United States v. Gray, 642 F.3d 371, 376–77 (2d Cir. 2011) (quoting Conn. Nat. Bank v. Germain, 503 U.S. 249, 254 (1992)).

10. 15 U.S.C. § 45(a)(1) (2006).

11. Americans with Disabilities Act of 1990 § 101(9), 42 U.S.C. § 12111(9) (2006).

12. Felix Frankfurter, *Some Reflections on the Reading of Statutes*, 47 COLUM. L. REV. 527, 543 (1947), *reprinted in* JUDGES ON JUDGING: VIEWS FROM THE BENCH 221, 229 (David M. O'Brien ed., 1997).

13. There is also an en banc procedure whereby the entire Court of Appeals—in the United States Court of Appeals for the Second Circuit, thirteen active judges and any senior judges who sat on the three-judge panel—will collectively consider the issues raised by the panel's decision. En banc proceedings are rare, especially in the Second Circuit, where, in some years, no cases are heard en banc.

14. 28 U.S.C. §§ 1346(b), 2671–80 (2000).

15. 28 U.S.C. § 1346(b)(1) (2006).

16. 28 U.S.C. § 2680(b) (2000).

17. Robinson v. United States, 849 F. Supp. 799, 802 (S.D. Ga. 1994).

18. Bono v. United States, 145 F. Supp. 2d 441, 446 (D.N.J. 2001).

19. Smith v. United States, 507 U.S. 197, 203 (1993) (quoting United States v. Kubrick, 444 U.S. 111, 117–18 (1979)).

20. Hughes Aircraft Co. v. Jacobson, 525 U.S. 432, 438 (1999).

21. Raila v. United States, 355 F.3d 118, 120 (2d Cir. 2004) (citing Saks v. Franklin Covey Co., 316 F.3d 337, 345 (2d Cir. 2003)).

22. *See* Dole v. United Steelworkers, 494 U.S. 26, 36 (1990); WILLIAM N. ESKRIDGE, JR., PHILIP P. FRICKEY & ELIZABETH GARRETT, LEGISLATION AND STATUTORY INTERPRETATION 253–55 (2000); 2A NORMAN J. SINGER, STATUTES AND STATUTORY CONSTRUCTION § 47:16 (6th ed. 2000).

23. *See* Kosak v. United States, 465 U.S. 848, 855 (1984).

24. 28 U.S.C. § 2680(*l*).

25. 28 U.S.C. § 2680(m).

26. 28 U.S.C. § 2680(c).

27. *Kosak*, 465 U.S. at 855 (emphasis in original).

28. H.R. REP. NO. 77-2245, at 10 (1942).

29. *Hearings on S. 2690 Before a Subcomm. of the S. Comm. on the Judiciary*, 76th Cong. 38 (1940) (testimony of A. Holtzoff, Special Assistant to the Attorney General of the United States).

30. Birnbaum v. United States, 436 F. Supp. 967, 974 (E.D.N.Y. 1977), *rev'd in part*, 588 F.2d 319 (2d Cir. 1978).

31. Dolan v. U.S. Postal Serv., 377 F.3d 285, 287–88 (3d Cir. 2004) (citation omitted).

32. Dolan v. U.S. Postal Serv., 546 U.S. 481, 486 (2006).
33. *Dolan*, 546 U.S. at 486 (quoting Jarecki v. G.D. Searle & Co., 367 U.S. 303, 307 (1961)).
34. *Dolan*, 546 U.S. at 490 (quoting *Kosak*, 465 U.S. at 855).
35. *Dolan*, 546 U.S. at 491 (quoting Lane v. Peña, 518 U.S. 187, 192 (1996)).
36. *Dolan*, 546 U.S. at 492 (quoting United States v. Yellow Cab Co., 340 U.S. 543, 547 (1951)).
37. *Dolan*, 546 U.S. at 493–94 (Thomas, J., dissenting) (footnote and citation omitted).
38. Abbe R. Gluck & Lisa Schultz Bressman, *Statutory Interpretation from the Inside—An Empirical Study of Congressional Drafting, Delegation, and the Canons: Part I*, 65 STAN. L. REV. 901, 931–33 (2013).
39. RICHARD A. POSNER, THE FEDERAL COURTS: CRISIS AND REFORM 286 (1985).
40. POSNER, CRISIS AND REFORM *supra* note 39, at 287. Judge Posner is of the view that "[g]ood pragmatic judges balance two types of consequence, the case-specific and the systemic." RICHARD A. POSNER, HOW JUDGES THINK 202–03 (2008); *see also* RICHARD A. POSNER, LAW, PRAGMATISM, AND DEMOCRACY 57–96 (2003) (promoting legal pragmatism, which "involves consideration of systemic and not just case-specific consequences"). Judge Posner endorses Learned Hand's view that judges should reconstruct imaginatively the legislature's purposes. *See* Learned Hand, *The Contribution of an Independent Judiciary to Civilization, in* MASS. BAR ASS'N, THE SUPREME JUDICIAL COURT OF MASSACHUSETTS 1692–1942, at 59 (1942), *reprinted in* THE SPIRIT OF LIBERTY: PAPERS AND ADDRESSES OF LEARNED HAND 155, 157 (Irving Dilliard ed., 3d ed. 1960) ("Courts must reconstruct the past solution imaginatively in its setting and project the purposes which inspired it upon the concrete occasions which arise for their decision.").
41. *See* United States v. Ingram, 164 F. Supp. 2d 310, 316–17 (N.D.N.Y. 2001).
42. Pub. L. No. 90-618, 82 Stat. 1213 (1968) (codified as amended at 18 U.S.C. §§ 921–31).
43. 18 U.S.C. § 922(g)(1) (emphasis added).
44. *See* Small v. United States, 333 F.3d 425, 427–28 (3d Cir. 2003); United States v. Atkins, 872 F.2d 94, 96 (4th Cir. 1989); United States v. Winson, 793 F.2d 754, 757–59 (6th Cir. 1986); United States v. Jalbert, 242 F. Supp. 2d 44, 47 (D. Me. 2003); United States v. Chant, Nos. CR 94-1149, CR 94-0185, 1997 WL 231105, at *1–3 (N.D. Cal. Apr. 4, 1997).
45. *See* United States v. Concha, 233 F.3d 1249, 1253–56 (10th Cir. 2000).
46. United States v. Martinez, 122 F.3d 421, 424 (7th Cir. 1997) (finding a military court to be included within "any court").
47. United States v. Gayle, 342 F.3d 89, 95 (2d Cir. 2003) (citations omitted).
48. 18 U.S.C. § 921(a)(20)(A) (emphasis added).
49. *Concha*, 233 F.3d at 1254.

50. *Gayle*, 342 F.3d at 93 (citing Marvel Characters, Inc. v. Simon, 310 F.3d 280, 290 (2d Cir. 2002), for the proposition that courts should be reluctant to read a statute in a way that could "lead to anomalous or unreasonable results").

51. *Gayle*, 342 F.3d at 93–94 (citing United States v. Nelson, 277 F.3d 164, 186 (2d Cir. 2002)).

52. *Gayle*, 342 F.3d at 94 (quoting Disabled in Action of Metro. N.Y. v. Hammons, 202 F.3d 110, 124 (2d Cir. 2000)).

53. S. REP. No. 90-1501, at 31 (1968).

54. *Gayle*, 342 F.3d at 94 (quoting *Hammons*, 202 F.3d at 124).

55. H.R. REP. No. 90-1956, at 4, 8, 28–29 (1968) (Conf. Rep.).

56. The Conference Report provides:

> *Definition of crimes.*—Both the House bill and the Senate amendment prohibited the shipment, transportation, and receipt of firearms and ammunition by persons under indictment for, or convicted of, certain crimes.... A difference between the House bill and the Senate amendment which recurs in the provisions described above is that the crime referred to in the House bill is one punishable by imprisonment for more than 1 year and the crime referred to in the Senate Amendment is a crime of violence punishable as a felony.... The conference substitute adopts the crime referred to in the House bill (one punishable by imprisonment for more than 1 year)....

H.R. Rep. No. 90-1956, at 28–29.

57. *Gayle*, 342 F.3d at 96.

58. *Compare Gayle*, 342 F.3d at 95 ("convicted in any court" does not include foreign convictions), *and* United States v. Concha, 233 F.3d 1249, 1256 (10th Cir. 2000) (same), *with* Small v. United States, 333 F.3d 425, 427–28 (3d Cir. 2003) ("convicted in any court" includes foreign convictions), United States v. Atkins, 872 F.2d 94, 96 (4th Cir. 1989) (same), *and* United States v. Winson, 793 F.2d 754, 757–59 (6th Cir. 1986) (same).

59. Small v. United States, 544 U.S. 385, 388 (2005) (citations omitted).

60. *Small*, 544 U.S. at 388–89 (citing Foley Bros., Inc. v. Filardo, 336 U.S. 281, 285 (1949)).

61. *Small*, 544 U.S. at 390.

62. *Small*, 544 U.S. at 391, 393.

63. *Small*, 544 U.S. at 397 (Thomas, J., dissenting) (footnote omitted).

64. *Small*, 544 U.S. at 398 (Thomas, J., dissenting) (citations omitted).

65. *Small*, 544 U.S. at 403 (Thomas, J., dissenting) (citation omitted).

66. *Small*, 544 U.S. at 407 (Thomas, J., dissenting).

67. *Small*, 544 U.S. at 407 (Thomas, J., dissenting).

68. 20 U.S.C. § 1415(i)(3)(B)(i).

69. Murphy v. Arlington Cent. Sch. Dist. Bd. of Educ., 402 F.3d 332, 336 (2d Cir. 2005).
70. 499 U.S. 83 (1991), *abrogated by statute*, 42 U.S.C. § 1988(c).
71. Crawford Fitting Co. v. J.T. Gibbons, Inc., 482 U.S. 437, 439 (1987).
72. *Casey*, 499 U.S. at 87, 102.
73. *Casey*, 499 U.S. at 91 n.5 (quoting H.R. Rep. No. 99-687, at 5 (1986) (Conf. Rep.), *reprinted in* 1986 U.S.C.C.A.N. 1807, 1808 (omission in original)).
74. *Casey*, 499 U.S. at 91 n.5 (emphasis in original).
75. *Murphy*, 402 F.3d at 337 (citing the Civil Rights Act of 1991 Pub. L. No. 102-166, § 113, 105 Stat. 1071, 1079 (codified as amended at 42 U.S.C., § 1988)).
76. *Murphy*, 402 F.3d at 337 n.6 (citing the Individuals with Disabilities Education Improvement Act of 2004, Pub. L. No. 108-446, 118 Stat. 2647 (codified as amended in scattered sections of 20 U.S.C.), the Education Flexibility Partnership Act of 1999, Pub. L. No. 106-25, 113 Stat. 41 (codified as amended at 20 U.S.C. §§ 1415, 5891a, 5891b), and the IDEA Amendments of 1997, Pub. L. No. 105-17, 111 Stat. 37 (codified as amended at 20 U.S.C. §§ 1400–1481)).
77. 20 U.S.C. § 1400(d)(1)(A), (B).
78. 20 U.S.C. § 1415(h)(1).
79. 20 U.S.C. § 1415(i)(3)(B).
80. Our panel also held prospectively that a plaintiff's application for fees for experts or consultants who perform services in IDEA actions will normally not be approved unless the application is accompanied by time records contemporaneously maintained by the person performing the services. *Murphy*, 402 F.3d at 339.
81. *See* Arons v. N.J. State Bd. of Educ., 842 F.2d 58 (3d Cir. 1988).
82. *See* T.D. v. LaGrange Sch. Dist. No. 102, 349 F.3d 469, 482 (7th Cir. 2003); Neosho R–V Sch. Dist. v. Clark, 315 F.3d 1022, 1031 (8th Cir. 2003).
83. Arlington Cent. Sch. Dist. Bd. of Educ. v. Murphy, 548 U.S. 291, 304 (2006).
84. *Arlington Cent. Sch. Dist.*, 548 U.S. at 302–03.
85. *Arlington Cent. Sch. Dist.*, 548 U.S. at 305–06 (Ginsburg, J., concurring in part).
86. *Arlington Cent. Sch. Dist.*, 548 U.S. at 308–09 (Breyer, J., dissenting) (citation omitted).
87. *Arlington Cent. Sch. Dist.*, 548 U.S. at 323–24 (Breyer, J., dissenting).
88. *Arlington Cent. Sch. Dist.*, 548 U.S. at 324 (Breyer, J., dissenting) (citation omitted).
89. *Arlington Cent. Sch. Dist.*, 548 U.S. at 308 (Souter, J., dissenting).
90. KENT GREENAWALT, STATUTORY AND COMMON LAW INTERPRETATION 140 (2013).

Chapter 6

1. *See* JAMES OLDHAM, ENGLISH COMMON LAW IN THE AGE OF MANSFIELD 31–32 (2004) (discussing Mansfield's legislative and judicial experience). For this reference, I am grateful to Professor Bernadette Meyler of Stanford Law School.

2. Magistrate Judge Edward G. Bryant of Tennessee was a member of the House of Representatives from Tennessee, and Judge Gregory Carman of the Court of International Trade was a member of the House of Representatives from New York. In the 1980s, judges who had been members of Congress included Frank M. Coffin, Abner J. Mikva, Thomas Meskill, James L. Buckley, Donald Russell, Oren Harris, Charles Wiggins, William Hungate, and Gregory Carman.

   Several federal judges have had substantial legislative experience as congressional staffers, including Justice Breyer, but they comprise a small percentage of the judiciary as a whole. On this point, I am grateful to Daniel Holt of the Federal Judicial Center's History Office, see e-mail from Richard Jaffe to author (Oct. 12, 2011, 17:50 EST) (on file with author), as well as to Judge Richard Eaton of the Court of International Trade, himself a former congressional chief of staff, and to Richard Jaffe of the Administrative Office of the U.S. Courts, for their insights.

3. Representative Alcee Hastings of Florida was a federal district court judge, and Senator John Cornyn of Texas was a Texas Supreme Court justice. Legislators who clerked for federal judges include Senator Richard Blumenthal of Connecticut, Senator Kirsten Gillibrand of New York, Senator Mike Lee of Utah, and Senator Ted Cruz of Texas.

4. M. DOUGLASS BELLIS, FED. JUDICIAL CTR., STATUTORY STRUCTURE AND LEGISLATIVE DRAFTING CONVENTIONS: A PRIMER FOR JUDGES (2008), *available at* http://www.fjc.gov/public/pdf.nsf/lookup/draftcon.pdf/$file/draftcon.pdf.

5. *See supra* Chapter Four, notes 77–81 and accompanying text.

6. JEREMY WALDRON, THE DIGNITY OF LEGISLATION 5 (1999).

7. *See* JUDICIAL CONFERENCE OF THE U.S., LONG RANGE PLAN FOR THE FEDERAL COURTS 126 (1995), *available at* http://www.uscourts.gov/uscourts/FederalCourts/Publications/FederalCourtsLongRangePlan.pdf (proposing a checklist of potential technical problems for use by legislative staff); JOSEPH F. WEIS, JR. ET AL., REPORT OF THE FEDERAL COURTS STUDY COMMITTEE 91–92 (1990), *available at* http://www.fjc.gov/public/pdf.nsf/lookup/repfcsc.pdf/$file/repfcsc.pdf (same); Peter H. Schuck, *Trimming Litigation*, AM. LAW., Dec. 2008, at 79 (discussing cost savings and other benefits of a checklist aimed at common, inadvertent problems with legislative drafting).

8. 28 U.S.C. § 1658(a) (2006). On statutory default rules, see EINER ELHAUGE, STATUTORY DEFAULT RULES (2008).

9. Ledbetter v. Goodyear Tire & Rubber Co., 550 U.S. 618, 661 (2007) (Ginsburg, J., dissenting) ("As in 1991, the Legislature may act to correct this Court's parsimonious reading of Title VII."); *see also*, e.g., Schindler Elevator Corp. v. United States *ex rel.* Kirk, 131 S. Ct. 1885, 1898 (2011) (Ginsburg, J., dissenting) ("After today's decision, which severely limits whistleblowers' ability to substantiate their allegations before commencing suit, that question is worthy of Congress' attention.").

10. *See* William N. Eskridge, Jr., *Overriding Supreme Court Statutory Interpretation Decisions,* 101 YALE L.J. 331, 334 (1991) ("Congress and its committees are aware of the Court's statutory decisions, devote significant efforts toward analyzing their policy implications, and override those decisions with a frequency heretofore unreported."); Matthew R. Christiansen & William N. Eskridge, Jr., *Congressional Overrides of Supreme Court Statutory Interpretation Decisions, 1967–2011,* TEX. L. REV. (forthcoming 2014) (updating Eskridge's landmark study); Michael E. Solimine & James L. Walker, *The Next Word: Congressional Response to Supreme Court Statutory Decisions,* 65 TEMP. L. REV. 425, 425–26 (1992) (noting Congress's willingness to override Supreme Court decisions with which it disagrees); JEFFREY A. SEGAL, HAROLD J. SPAETH & SARA C. BENESH, THE SUPREME COURT IN THE AMERICAN LEGAL SYSTEM 325 (2005) (noting that Congress does override Supreme Court decisions with some regularity). For a rich case study of how Congress responds to Supreme Court decisions, see Elizabeth Garrett, *The Story of* TVA v. Hill: *Congress Has the Last Word, in* STATUTORY INTERPRETATION STORIES (William N. Eskridge, Jr., Philip P. Frickey & Elizabeth Garrett eds.) 58 (New York: Foundation Press, 2011). On occasion, the Supreme Court invites Congress to review its statutory decisions. *See* Lori Hausegger & Lawrence Baum, *Inviting Congressional Action: A Study of Supreme Court Motivations in Statutory Interpretation,* 43 AM. J. POL. SCI. 162, 164 (1999) (noting that such invitations are diffuse or vague). On the impact of legislative polarization on congressional overrides, see, for example, Richard L. Hasen, *End of the Dialogue? Political Polarization, the Supreme Court, and Congress,* 86 S. CAL. L. REV. 205 (2013); Virginia A. Hettinger & Christopher Zorn, *Explaining the Incidence and Timing of Congressional Responses to the U.S. Supreme Court,* 30 LEGIS. STUD. Q. 5 (2005); and Adam Liptak, *In Congress's Paralysis, a Mightier Supreme Court,* N.Y. TIMES, Aug. 21, 2012, at A10, *available at* http://www.nytimes.com/2012/08/21/us/politics/supreme-court-gains-power-from-paralysis-of-congress.html?_r=0.

11. Ruth Bader Ginsburg, *Communicating and Commenting on the Court's Work,* 83 GEO. L.J. 2119, 2125 (1995).

12. Ginsburg, *supra* note 11.

13. HENRY J. FRIENDLY, *The Gap in Lawmaking—Judges Who Can't and Legislators Who Won't, in* BENCHMARKS 41, 49 (1967).

14. FRIENDLY, *supra* note 13, at 47.

15. FRIENDLY, *supra* note 13, at 47–48.

16. FRIENDLY, *supra* note 13, at 58.

17. James L. Buckley, Commentary, *The Perspective of a Judge and Former Legislator,* 85 GEO. L.J. 2223, 2224 (1997).

18. For a review of such mechanisms, especially in the states, see Shirley S. Abrahmson & Robert L. Hughes, *Shall We Dance? Steps For Legislators and Judges in Statutory Interpretation,* 75 MINN. L. REV. 1045, 1059–81 (1991), where the

authors discuss mechanisms for legislative monitoring of judicial opinions interpreting statutes.

19. Ruth Bader Ginsburg & Peter W. Huber, *The Intercircuit Committee*, 100 HARV. L. REV. 1417, 1428, 1432 (1987).

20. *Interview with Chief Judge Frank M. Coffin*, THIRD BRANCH (Admin. Office of the U.S. Courts, Washington, D.C.), June 1982, at 1, 6.

21. James L. Oakes, *Grace Notes on "Grace Under Pressure,"* 50 OHIO ST. L.J. 701, 714-15 (1989).

22. Wilfred Feinberg, *A National Court of Appeals?*, 42 BROOK. L. REV. 611, 627 (1976) (recognizing that if conflicts among the circuits can be brought to Congress's attention, then they may be easily resolved by a "formal expression of legislative intent").

23. *See* John Paul Stevens, *Some Thoughts on Judicial Restraint*, 66 JUDICATURE 177, 183 (1982) (discussing the efficiency and appropriateness of a congressional role in the resolution of intercircuit conflicts on questions of statutory construction).

24. Benjamin N. Cardozo, *A Ministry of Justice*, 35 HARV. L. REV. 113, 114 (1921) (citing Roscoe Pound, *Juristic Problems of National Progress*, 22 AM. J. SOC. 721, 729, 731 (1917); 9 THE WORKS OF JEREMY BENTHAM 597-612 (John Bowring ed., 1843)); *see also* Larry Kramer, *"The One-Eyed Are Kings": Improving Congress's Ability To Regulate the Use of Judicial Resources*, LAW & CONTEMP. PROBS., Summer 1991, at 73, 90-97 (1991) (discussing the need for an interbranch agency to reconcile discrepancies between Congress and the judiciary).

25. FRIENDLY, *supra* note 13, at 62.

26. *See supra* Preface note 3 and accompanying text (discussing the work of the Governance Institute).

27. Ginsburg & Huber, *supra* note 19, at 1428.

28. Here, I draw upon Robert A. Katzmann & Russell R. Wheeler, *A Mechanism for "Statutory Housekeeping": Appellate Courts Working with Congress*, 9 J. APP. PRAC. & PROCESS 131 (2007) (arguing that Congress finds the program helpful because it alerts Congress and its statute drafters to potential drafting problems).

29. At the time, I was president of the Governance Institute and a Brookings Institution fellow, and taught at Georgetown.

30. Proceedings of the Forty-Ninth Judiciary Conference of the D.C. Circuit, 124 F.R.D. 241, 312-36 (1988).

31. ROBERT A. KATZMANN, COURTS AND CONGRESS 73-74 (1997).

32. KATZMANN, *supra* note 31, at 76-77 (noting the meeting between congressional members and D.C. Circuit Judges Wald, Buckley, Ginsburg, and Mikva).

33. *See* William H. Rehnquist, *Chief Justice Issues 1992 Year-End Report*, THIRD BRANCH (Admin. Office of the U.S. Courts, Washington, D.C.), Jan. 1993, at 1, 5-6 (noting that the Supreme Court decided in 1993 to make the pilot project permanent).

34. *See* JUDICIAL CONFERENCE OF THE U.S., *supra* note 7, at 127 (describing the project in Implementation Strategy 91e). The early days of the project were the subject of a special report in the *Georgetown Law Journal*. *See* Robert A. Katzmann & Stephanie M. Herseth, Special Report, *An Experiment in Statutory Communication Between Courts and Congress: A Progress Report*, 85 GEO. L.J. 2189 (1997). The issue included individual commentaries by M. Douglass Bellis, Frank L. Burk, Jr., Mark J. Langer, and Judge James L. Buckley. *See* M. Douglass Bellis, Commentary, *A View from the House of Representatives*, 85 GEO. L.J. 2209 (1997); Frank Burk, Commentary, *Statutory Housekeeping: A Senate Perspective*, 85 GEO. L.J. 2217 (1997); Mark J. Langer, Commentary, *Implementing the Project: A Court Administrator's Role*, 85 GEO. L.J. 2219 (1997); James L. Buckley, Commentary, *The Perspective of a Judge and Former Legislator*, 85 GEO. L.J. 2223 (1997).

35. The offices of legislative counsel in the House and the Senate are nonpartisan units that provide confidential drafting services requested by individual legislators and legislative committees. *See* OFFICE OF THE LEGISLATIVE COUNSEL, U.S. HOUSE OF REPRESENTATIVES, http://www.house.gov/legcoun/(last visited Oct. 4, 2013); OFFICE OF THE LEGISLATIVE COUNSEL, U.S. SENATE, http://slc.senate.gov/index.htm (last visited Oct. 4, 2013). Background of the legislative counsels' interest in the project is set forth in Memorandum from James C. Duff, Dir., Admin. Office of the U.S. Courts, Judge D. Brock Hornby, U.S. Dist. Court for the Dist. of Me., & Judge Robert A. Katzmann, U.S. Court of Appeals for the Second Circuit, to Judges, U.S. Courts of Appeal, and Clerks of Court, U.S. Courts of Appeal, Project To Provide Congress with Appellate Opinions Bearing on Technical Matters of Statutory Construction 1, 2 (July 19, 2007) [hereinafter Memorandum from Duff, Hornby & Katzmann] (on file with author).

36. Memorandum from Duff, Hornby & Katzmann, *supra* note 35. From time to time, the Administrative Office and the leadership of the Committee on the Judicial Branch provide updates about the project. *See, e.g.*, Memorandum from Judge John D. Bates, Dir., Admin. Office of the U.S. Courts & Judge Robert A. Katzmann, U.S. Court of Appeals for the Second Circuit, to Judges, U.S. Courts of Appeal, and Clerks of Court, U.S. Courts of Appeal, Project To Provide Congress with Appellate Opinions Bearing on Technical Matters of Statutory Construction (Aug. 15, 2013) (on file with author).

37. *See* Memorandum from Russell R. Wheeler, President, Governance Institute, Statutory Housekeeping Project (July 3, 2013) (on file with author) (providing a list and description of cases).

38. *See* Rotimi v. Holder, 577 F.3d 133, 134 (2d Cir. 2009) (upholding a Board of Immigration Appeals decision which held that an applicant for a waiver of inadmissibility had not "lawfully resided continuously" in the United States as required by the statute during the period in which his visitor visa had expired, and noting that the fact that the applicant had applied for asylum and for adjustment of status had no bearing).

39. *See* Ross-Tousey v. Neary (*In re* Ross-Tousey), 549 F.3d 1148, 1150 (7th Cir. 2008) (holding that "an above-median-income debtor who has no monthly vehicle loan or lease payment can claim a vehicle ownership expense deduction when calculating...disposable income"). *But see* Ransom v. MBNA, Am. Bank, N.A. (*In re* Ransom), 577 F.3d 1026, 1031–32 (9th Cir. 2009) (holding that a debtor is not entitled to a vehicle ownership expense deduction for a vehicle that he owns free and clear of liens). In January 2011, the Supreme Court held that car owners who do not make loan or lease payments are not entitled to the deduction. *See* Ransom v. FIA Card Servs., N.A., 131 S. Ct. 716, 730 (2011).

40. *See* United States v. Dixon, 551 F.3d 578, 582–83 (7th Cir. 2008) (holding that section 2250 of the Act does not require that the defendant's travel postdate the Act), *rev'd sub nom.* Carr v. United States, 130 S. Ct. 2229 (2010).

41. *See* Carr v. United States, 130 S. Ct. 2229, 2242 (2010) (holding that section 2250 does not apply to sex offenders whose interstate travel occurred before the Sex Offender Registration and Notification Act's effective date).

42. *See* United States v. Vasquez, 611 F.3d 325, 328 (7th Cir. 2010) (holding that the government was not required to prove that the defendant had specific knowledge that he was required to register under the Sex Offender Registration and Notification Act).

43. Class Action Fairness Act of 2005, Pub. L. No. 109-2, 119 Stat. 4 (codified as amended in scattered sections of 28 U.S.C.).

44. 28 U.S.C. § 1453(c)(1) (2006) (amended 2009).

45. Morgan v. Gay, 466 F.3d 276, 277 (3d Cir. 2006).

46. Spivey v. Vertrue, Inc., 528 F.3d 982, 983–84 (7th Cir. 2008) (noting that an imprecisely stated deadline in the statute does not constitute a sufficient basis for courts to simply disregard the language of the actual statute).

47. Statutory Time-Periods Technical Amendments Act of 2009, Pub. L. No. 111-16, 123 Stat. 1607, 1608 (to be codified at 28 U.S.C. § 1453(c)(1)).

48. Memorandum from Duff, Hornby & Katzmann, *supra* note 35, at 3 attach.1.

49. Memorandum from Duff, Hornby & Katzmann, *supra* note 35, at 3 attach.1.

50. *See* Memorandum from Duff, Hornby & Katzmann, *supra* note 35, at 2 ("[T]he opinions help Congress understand how statutes may be drafted to make legislative intent as clear as possible.... The House and Senate legislative counsel... are principally responsible for analyzing the drafting issues identified in each opinion....").

51. Memorandum from Duff, Hornby & Katzmann, *supra* note 35, at 2.

52. *See* Bellis, *supra* note 34, at 2209 (noting that the House Office of Legislative Counsel has been "involved with the project since its inception"); Burk, *supra* note 34, at 2217 (noting that the Senate Office of Legislative Counsel's participation in the project "has been a success").

53. *See, e.g.,* Letter from Rep. Thomas S. Foley, Speaker of the U.S. House of Representatives, Sen. Richard A. Gephardt, Majority Leader of the U.S. Senate & Sen. Robert H. Michel, Republican Leader of the U.S. Senate, to David

Meade, Legislative Counsel (Sept. 28, 1992), *in Interbranch Relations: Hearings Before the Joint Comm. on the Org. of Cong.*, 103d Cong. 76, 309 (1993); Letter from Sen. George J. Mitchell, Majority Leader of the U.S. Senate, Sen. Robert Dole, Republican Leader of the U.S. Senate & Sen. Robert C. Byrd, President Pro Tempore of the U.S. Senate, to Frank L. Burk, Jr., Legislative Counsel for the U.S. Senate, *in Interbranch Relations, supra,* at 310; H.R. REP. NO. 103-413(I), at 25 (1993) (encouraging "the appropriate committees of jurisdiction in the House and Senate to monitor regularly and systematically Federal court decisions and to report periodically to their respective Chambers on the significant issues that merit review in this relationship"); S. REP. NO. 103-215(I) (1993); Letter from Rep. John Conyers, Jr., Chairman, H. Comm. on the Judiciary & Rep. Lamar S. Smith, Ranking Member, H. Comm. on the Judiciary, to M. Pope Barrow, Legislative Counsel for the U.S. House of Representatives, at 2 (May 23, 2007) (on file with author)(recommending that the House Office of Legislative Counsel "continue its participation in the project") [hereinafter Conyers & Smith Letter]; Letter from Sen. Orrin Hatch, Chairman, S. Comm. on the Judiciary & Sen. Patrick Leahy, Ranking Democratic Member, S. Comm. on the Judiciary, to James Fransen, Legislative Counsel for the U.S. Senate (Mar. 21, 2001) (on file with author); Letter from Sen. Patrick Leahy, Chairman, S. Comm. on the Judiciary & Arlen Specter, Ranking Republican Member, S. Comm. on the Judiciary, to James Fransen, Legislative Counsel for the U.S. Senate (Feb. 14, 2007) [hereinafter Leahy & Specter Letter] (on file with author) (recommending that the Senate Office of Legislative Counsel "continue its participation in the project").

54. E-mail from Danielle Cutrona, Chief Nominations Counsel for Sen. Jeff Sessions, S. Comm. on the Judiciary, to author (Sept. 14, 2010, 10:41 EST) (on file with author) (indicating Senator Jeff Sessions's remarks to the Judiciary).

55. Burk, *supra* note 34, at 2217.

56. Burk, *supra* note 34, at 2217.

57. *See Feedback Requested on Technical Aspects of Law,* THIRD BRANCH (Admin. Office of the U.S. Courts, Washington, D.C.), Aug. 2007, at 7, 9, *available at* http://www.uscourts.gov/News/TheThirdBranch/07-08-01/Feedback_Requested_on_Technical_Aspects_of_Laws.aspx (discussing Fransen's belief in the usefulness of the project).

58. *Feedback Requested on Technical Aspects of Law, supra* note 57.

59. Bellis, *supra* note 34, at 2215.

60. Katzmann & Wheeler, *supra* note 28, at 140.

61. Bellis, *supra* note 34, at 2213.

62. Bellis, *supra* note 34, at 2213.

63. Robert Katzmann & Russell R. Wheeler, *More About the "Statutory Housekeeping Project,"* IN CAMERA (Fed. Judges Ass'n), Aug. 31, 2010, *available at* http://www.federaljudgesassoc.org/egov/docs/newsletters/38_167_716.asp;

Feedback on Technical Matters Aids Legislation, THIRD BRANCH (Admin. Office of the U.S. Courts, Washington, D.C.), Feb. 2010, at 4, *available at* http://www. uscourts.gov/News/TheThirdBranch/TTBViewer.aspx?doc=/uscourts/news/ttb/archive/2010-02%20Feb.pdf.

64. Conyers & Smith Letter, *supra* note 53; Leahy & Specter Letter, *supra* note 53.

65. The Administrative Conference of the United States, currently chaired by the well-known legal scholar and administrator, Paul Verkuil, is an independent federal agency dedicated to improving the administrative process. ADMIN. CONF. OF THE U.S., http://www.acus.gov/ (last visited Oct. 4, 2013).

66. For these suggestions, I am grateful to Professor Charnovitz of George Washington University Law School and former legislative assistant to two Speakers of the House of Representatives. E-mail from Steven Charnovitz, Associate Professor of Law, George Washington University School of Law, to author (Mar. 30, 2014, 11:39 A.M. EST) (on file with author).

67. *See* Stephen F. Ross, *Where Have You Gone Karl Llewellyn? Should Congress Turn Its Lonely Eyes to You?,* 45 VAND. L. REV. 561, 575–76 (1992).

68. Robert A. Katzmann, *Summary of Proceedings, in* JUDGES AND LEGISLATORS: TOWARD INSTITUTIONAL COMITY 162, 167 (Robert A. Katzmann ed., 1988).

69. Orrin Hatch, *Legislative History: Tool of Construction or Destruction,* 11 HARV. J.L. & PUB. POL'Y 43, 48 (1988).

Conclusion

1. THE FEDERALIST NO. 62, at 445 (James Madison) (Pocket Books ed. 2004).

INDEX